AT HOME ON HOTHAM HILL

from Lorna Hannan

The Annals of Hotham
Volume 4

AT HOME ON HOTHAM HILL

A portrait of a nineteenth century entrepreneur

GUY MURPHY

THE HOTHAM HISTORY PROJECT 2004

Hotham History Project
C/- North Melbourne Library
Errol Street, North Melbourne, Victoria, 3051

Published with the assistance of the City of Melbourne.

First published August 2004

National Library of Australia Cataloguing-in-Publication entry

Murphy, Guy.

The annals of Hotham. Volume 4, At home on Hotham hill : portrait of a nineteenth century entrepreneur.

Bibliography.
Includes index.
ISBN 0 9586111 5 7.

1. Langford, Robert, 1847- . 2. Langford family. 3. Mayors - Victoria - North Melbourne - Biography. 4. North Melbourne (Vic.) - Biography. I. Hotham History Project. II. Title.

320.854092

Edited by Bet Moore

Layout, cover design and production by
Pauline McClenahan
Captured Concepts, St Andrews, Vic 3761

Printed by BPA Books, Melbourne

Front cover: 519 Dryburgh Street, 1988. Painting by Eliza Szarukan.

The author is interested in hearing from anyone with old photographs and other historic documents relating to 519 Dryburgh Street or Robert Langford. He may be contacted C/- the North Melbourne Library.

Contents

For my grandmother
Ruth Wright

Foreword

For more than a century, countless passers-by have wondered about the big house at 519 Dryburgh Street, North Melbourne—the house with the overgrown Bougainvillea and the commanding view of Royal Park. Who lives there now, who built it, what are its stories? Guy Murphy has more than answered those questions and many more.

This history of a house and its owners and tenants covers more than a hundred and fifty years, and encapsulates the history of Melbourne, its commercial life, its property speculation and development, its hard times, and its renewal. This is a marvellous piece of historical research, with scarcely a stone left unturned from the history of early Melbourne's markets and fish trade, to property speculation, family history and the boarding house business. We meet many of the people who have made it their home, in particular its primary builder Robert Langford, who rose from fish-hawker to man of property and civic leader.

This study is an important piece of economic history that illuminates the way people made money in colonial Victoria, and how that new wealth fuelled the boom that made Melbourne one of the great cities of the nineteenth century world. It also provides a micro-history of the creation of slum housing through the sub-division of lots of land into tiny properties that were doomed, until recent times, to be dark, damp and over-crowded. We see how one man's wealth supported his extended family in small sub-divisions nearby, perpetuating the extended household where families had traditionally maintained their less affluent relatives. The rich childless couple lived in the grand two-story house; the less successful parents and siblings, some with many children, were relegated to the adjoining cottages and a villa. We follow the house's decline after the financial crash of the 1890s, until 1923, when it could be bought by a stevedore for twenty gold sovereigns. Dryburgh and Curran streets were by then depressed and poor, and the big houses served to provide accommodation for those without families, or those passing through. Not until 1968 did it return to being a family home, when its current owner began to renovate it.

Houses cannot tell their own stories: that depends on the skill of the historian, and this history of the house with the purple creeper is destined to be a classic.

Janet McCalman
North Melbourne

Acknowledgments

This book began as a short university assignment: dating the construction of a house. It was to turn into something much bigger. Researching and writing it has been a wonderful education in historic research methods, and I wish to thank many people who have helped me along the way.

I will begin by thanking the Committee of the Hotham History Project, including Lorna Hannan, Mary Kehoe, Rae Nichols and Felicity Jack, whose collective support has facilitated this volume coming into being. Winsome Roberts deserves special thanks both for her encouragement and for drawing my attention to the large body of material in the *North Melbourne Advertiser*, which inspired me to broaden the scope of the study.

Heather McKay, Local History Librarian at the North Melbourne Library, provided me with ongoing help over a period of many years, directing me to newly discovered sources of information, and putting me in touch with other researchers.

My thanks also goes to the staff of the State Library of Victoria, Lands Victoria, the Gravesend Central Library in Kent, and the Public Records Office of Victoria for much generous assistance.

My quest for information about Robert Langford was complicated by the fact that he and his wife Elizabeth had no surviving children. The descendants of other branches of the Langford family have helped bridge this gap by being wonderfully supportive and forthcoming with privately held material – special mention goes to Kaye Carr, Margaret Pike, Diane McDonald, Walter Claringbold and Robyn Lorenz. Members of other families who have lived at 519 Dryburgh Street have also provided me with information. These include Robert Cannon, Andre Wright, Adrian Ringrose and Pauline McGuffie.

I wish to express appreciation to the copyright holders of all the images included in this edition, for granting me permission to reproduce. I particularly want to thank

Eliza Szarukan for kindly allowing me to reproduce her beautiful artwork on the front cover.

I want to thank the City of Melbourne for supporting the publication of this book.

Thank you to my employer Peter Lovell for giving me the opportunity to learn so much about historic research methodology and the history of Melbourne, which has led this to be a much richer volume. My appreciation also goes to my colleague Jean-Anne Wells for her advice relating to interior decoration.

The transformation of my manuscript into a book has very much been a Curran Street affair. Thank you to Janet McCalman for taking the time to read the text and write the preface.

Bet Moore kindly donated her expertise as an editor, and put us in touch with Pauline McClenahan, who has done an excellent job in laying out the book and designing the cover. Above all, Hugh O'Neill, owner of 519 Dryburgh Street, deserves special thanks for contributing his photography, and for his monumental patience and unflagging support over the past eight years.

1
Gravesend and the voyage out

On the first day of spring in 1884, Robert Langford held a housewarming party to celebrate the completion of his new home, Milton Hall. The party had to be moved to North Melbourne Town Hall after Robert invited 180 guests. According to the local newspaper the *North Melbourne Advertiser*, Langford's house on the corner of Dryburgh and Curran Streets was 'one of the most handsome structures in town', while a local councillor described it as 'an ornament and credit to the locality'.

Who was Robert Langford? Why did he build Milton Hall? What was the building like architecturally? To start to answer these questions, we really need to move back in time, three decades earlier to a seaside town on the other side of the world

~

Robert Langford was born in Gravesend, Kent, in the middle of the 19th century. In his childhood it was a town of grey slate roofs and three- and four-storey brick houses, with a population of around 16 000.[1] Thirty kilometres east of central London on the southern side of the Thames, Gravesend is old enough to have been mentioned in the Doomsday Book. There are remains of Roman settlements nearby. On the northern side of the river is Tilbury where Henry VIII built fortifications. The town straddled the boundary between Milton and Gravesend parishes, a third of the inhabitants living in Milton on the eastern side. A 19th century writer described it as 'an ancient, most fish-like town'.[2]

On account of its geography Gravesend has long had maritime connections with the outside world. The American Indian chief's daughter Pocohontus was buried in the grounds of St George's Church in 1616 after dying aboard ship on her way back to Virginia. Conveniently, the town lies exactly one tide away from London. Shipbuilding had been confined to small fishing boats until 1780, when William Cleverly established large new dockyards that began producing warships, sloops, frigates, gunboats and chain ships.[3] Vessels were built here for the East India

Company, which provisioned its ships at Gravesend. The dockyards became major economic providers for the town, which also became popular amongst holidaying Londoners in the early 19th century.

Town Pier Square was the focus of the town, overlooking one of several large piers along the waterfront.[4] Radiating from the square parallel to the river were East and West Streets, crammed with inns, hotels and other licensed houses serving visiting sailors, soldiers and townsfolk. Charles Dickens was a visitor to the area and would sometimes stay at one of the river-front hotels. There were also grocery shops, and fishmongers selling brown shrimps, herring, kipper and haddock. High Street led south from the square, its shops lined with trademen's signs. The predominantly timber buildings along the waterfront around High Street were periodically subject to rapidly spreading fires, a major outbreak occurring in 1857.

Amongst the public buildings on the north side of town was the Town Hall, a few blocks south along High Street. It had a classical facade, the pediment topped by figures representing Minerva, Truth and Justice. The market behind, one of the oldest in England, had originally been in an open square, on either side of which were built two covered ways supported by stone columns. A fish market was added to one side in 1829.[5] There was a hospital, post office and a joint stock bank. Libraries included The Literary Institution with its Ionic portico, and the less formal Penny's Library, popular with visitors and locals. All the main streets were paved. The railway station was built in the centre of town in 1849, connecting Gravesend with London to the west and the Kent coasts and Maidstone to the east. The locality had half a dozen churches, the tower of St George's a landmark of the town centre.

Overlooking Gravesend is Windmill Hill. 'There can have been fewer grander maritime sights than to witness from the summit of the hill in the mid-years of the 19th century the stately towers of square sail of the numerous clippers making their way up the river with cargoes of tea or grain, or wood or spice, after having been blown across the oceans of the world.'[6] A constant traffic of ships carrying emigrants also travelled east in the opposite direction, out towards the open sea. To the south was the water pumping station with its distinctive square chimney, beyond which lay open countryside.

Robert Langford's father John Langford was originally from Northfleet, a small village a short distance to the west. He was working as a fisherman when he married Robert's mother Harriet Anne Sherbert there in 1843, later becoming a labourer, grocer and a 'general trader'. Their first child, Alfred John, was born in 1847. Four more children followed; Robert on 9 May 1849, John Richard in 1851, James William in 1852 and Harriet Anne Moxham in 1856. Robert was probably named after his paternal grandfather, Harriet after her mother.

This Anglican family, who were able to afford a housekeeper, lived at 27 Clarence Street at the south edge of town, near Windmill Hill. It was then a neighbourhood of new houses, with wheatfields, orchards and market gardens to the south. There were 'a number of small eating houses convenient to the humbler classes, where coffee, tea and shrimps [were] supplied at a small expense'.[7] In Peppercroft Street to the east was a brickfield. Residences of the affluent scattered around the outskirts included nearby Baynard Castle, the large castellated gothic home of a former mayor. On the eastern side of town was the garrisoned New Tavern Fort. The older children probably attended the day school around the corner at Parrock Street. It also served as a church on Sundays until nearby Christ Church was built in 1856 – John Langford knew Mr Bayns, the church warden. Several other Langfords are listed in local directories from the mid-1840s, suggesting the family may have had relatives living close by.

Being a resort town, Gravesend provided vivid experiences for children. Windmill Hill was a recreation ground, with refreshment houses, donkey rides, goat-drawn chaises and other carnival activities. Tulley's Bazaar, a few streets away from the house, featured illuminated porthole views of Italy and Switzerland on the sides of the building, free orchestral music, and souvenirs for sale to tourists. The older Langford children probably went swimming at the oriental style Clifton Baths by the river, and visited the various pleasure gardens around the town. They would have watched steam trains pull in at the station and seen clipper ships berth at the piers.

The family left for Australia in late 1857. Several factors may have determined the choice to go to Australia rather than the United States or Canada. With the start of the gold rushes, the rapidly growing colony of Victoria had developed a reputation for economic opportunity. They may have heard favourable reports from friends or relatives already living there. The stream of traffic east along the Thames was a daily advertisement for the possibility of a new life elsewhere. A probable factor was that John Langford was able to secure work aboard the *Norfolk* as a passenger steward for the longer journey to Melbourne. Australian colonial governments were actively recruiting for migrants in Britain throughout the 1850s, with programs of assisted passage bringing 230 000 people to Australia in that decade.[8] While the rest of the family are listed as unassisted passengers, their travel may have been subsidised by the shipping company.

During the 1850s travel on the long route between England and Australia was by wooden ship, steamships then being too slow and requiring regular coaling stations.[9] The fastest ships were North American clippers, which in the 1850s set new speed records in the Great Southern Ocean. Shipping lines operating these vessels in the routes to Australia included the White Star and Black Ball Lines sailing from Liverpool. From London the Money Wigram & Sons and Blackwall Line of Packets carried cargoes using mainly smaller frigates built in the Blackwall Yard in London.

The *Norfolk* was one of the fastest ships operated by Money Wigram, a new 953-ton wooden barque built by Blackwall.[10] It had already made one return voyage to Melbourne. There were first, second and third class cabins, second class including

Gravesend from the north side of the Thames in the early 19th century. The windmill on Windmill Hill is visible at centre. The spire of St George's church is at the far right.
SOURCE: GRAVESEND LIBRARY

steward's services. The ship departed London on 26 November, the family most likely embarking at Gravesend, from where it sailed at 4 pm on 28 November.

John Langford took with him a character reference from the local community.

> John Langford has been a resident of this Borough upwards of Twenty Years, is married and has a family of five children, and has maintained the same by his persevering industry and hard labor in a creditable manner, and we know him to be of honest principles and of steady and sober habits, and most willing to fulfil the satisfaction of any Gentlemen, Merchant or Tradesmen who might desire to give him employment in any place that would require care, confidence and activity, and that he is peaceful and good disposed in his general conduct.
>
> We ... do hereby most willingly present him with this our recommendation, and in doing so give him our most hearty wishes for his welfare, in whatever portion of the Colony he may be induced to venture his humble fortunes. [11]

Amongst the undersigned were the local surgeon, the mayor, the postmaster, the rate collector and the superintendent of police.

The ship passed Plymouth on 1 December, encountering a southerly gale for two days, then light southerly and south-east winds for the next week.[12] Aboard were 25 cabin passengers, with about 125 others in the intermediate and steerage.[13] Conditions varied with cabin class and were lowest for the crew. Being a new ship, the *Norfolk* was probably more comfortable than most. Cabins were 'roomy, lofty and well ventilated',[14] but for most people accommodation would have been in the shallow roughly partitioned steerage space between the open deck and next deck below. Phillip Rayson, who made the same journey to Melbourne aboard the *Norfolk* in late 1858, wrote 'a voyage to Australia is sufficient punishment for any crime short of murder'.[15]

In most migrant ships families usually stayed in the central third of the steerage, in partitioned berths measuring 6 by 6 feet.[16] It was cramped, with no choice of the company, and no privacy. At night 'the singing and shouting of the sailors on deck and the creaking of the berths as the ship rolled from side to side made it impossible to sleep until one was thoroughly worn out'. Lighting was by candle or oil lamp, the area below deck being completely deprived of natural light in rough weather when all openings had to be closed. Sanitation usually consisted of a screened bucket. Vessels en route to Australia typically carried livestock.[17] 'On any part of the boards you are surrounded by the most villainous smells that ever assailed a nostril – your nose, your eyes and your ears are all offended.'[18]

The ship was legally required to supply and cook set quantities of food for each passenger. Geoffrey Blainey has described the typical diet on a migrant ship at this time.

> Each man or woman was given 10½ pounds of bulky food, of which five pounds were oatmeal, and the remainder rice, flour, bread or ship's biscuits. They were also allowed the weekly luxury of half a pound of sugar, two ounces of tea, and half a pound of molasses to spread on their bread or gruel. Children under 14 received half rations ... By 1855 the diets of most migrants had become more balanced with less oatmeal and flour and more meat. The weekly ration also had more variety and included 2 pounds of potatoes, 1½ pounds of

Robert Langford arrived with his family in 1858 aboard the *Norfolk*, believed to be the ship shown here. Launched by the shipping line Money Wigram & Sons to serve the London-Melbourne route, it was one of the fastest ships of its day.
SOURCE: STATE LIBRARY OF VICTORIA

> peas, ½ pound of raisins, 6 ounces of both suet and lime juice, 4 ounces of butter, one gill of vinegar, and a pinch of salt, pepper and mustard.[19]

The upper deck was available for exercise to help pass the time, but much depended on the weather and sea conditions. Cabin passengers might read, play cards, quoits and other games. Harriet Langford would have been busy looking after the children while her husband worked. There may have been congenial company amongst the other steerage passengers, and certainly playmates for the children, the older of whom would have particularly felt the tedium. Passengers frequently became seasick soon after the ship left the English Channel, some unlucky enough to be incapacitated for the entire journey.

The adults would have been aware of the risks associated with the voyage if they had read accounts of shipwrecks in English newspapers. Water would pour into the cabins when hatches were left open in rough weather. Rayson reported that 'our private cabin windows [were] under water when the ship rolled on one side and looking up at the clouds when it rolled on the other – such noises of utensils of every description flying about, breaking the crockery and bulging the tins'.

For a couple with small children there was the fear of disease, as typhus and scarlet fever could easily spread through the cramped living quarters. Although the ship did have a doctor, deaths were not unusual on board, even if only of natural causes. There was no fire for warmth or to dry clothes, and the stress of the living conditions and bleakness of the sea could be very depressing. 'I know nothing more subduing, more thoroughly crushing to the spirits ... than this constantly looking out on the dark heaving waters day after day, week after week, even to months, relieved by anything but strange looking birds ...'

On 10 December the ship would have been at about latitude 40°22' north and the equator was crossed on around 27 December. In the tropics 'the butter was oil and the salt in a swim, and if one leant against the partitions of our berths we stuck to the paint and flakes of it came off on our clothes'.[20] An awning over the deck provided a shaded place to sit and enjoy fresh air. It was particularly uncomfortable at night. 'We gasped for breath in our small berths, but we could get none, every window fastened and not a breath of any but the little that came down the gangway.'[21]

The meridian of the Cape of Good Hope was reached on 17 January. The fastest route between the Cape of Good Hope and Melbourne was not a straight line along the 38th parallel of latitude, but rather one that bowed far south to take advantage of the earth's curvature, saving over 1000 miles from the journey.[22] With the advent of chronometers, this Great Circle Route became the preferred course for ships travelling to Australia. The *Norfolk* would have taken this route, along which passengers sometimes saw icebergs and snowfalls while as far south as the Kerguelen Islands.

The most extreme weather conditions occurred along this stretch of ocean, such as in this description by Rayson.

> I had a great wish to see the sea in its wildest aspect, and the next day Pavissio assisted me to get on deck, the sight was an awfully grand one, you would fancy you were going to be swallowed up every moment when you were in the deep trough of the sea, but the noble ship would raise her head nobly to the clouds and ride over, dashing the spray on either side and rolling it behind in massive waves, she was the sport and conqueror of the mighty ocean. The waves broke so rapidly over her that we got thoroughly baptised before we got into our cabin again. [23]

Australia was finally sighted at noon on 7 February, when the blue streak of the Otways came into view. The ship reached Port Phillip Bay later that day. 'There was much bustle on board, cording boxes, sewing up beds etc.' The journey from Gravesend to Melbourne had taken a near record 71 days. The arrival was reported in the *Argus*.

> The celebrated Blackwell liner *Norfolk*, commanded by Captain E. A. Reynells (late of the *True Britain*), arrived at Port Phillip Heads on Sunday, 7th inst., at 10 p.m., and received her pilot, but owing to contrary winds, she was unable to enter the Heads until 4 p.m. the next day. ... Immediately at the *Norfolk* being telegraphed at the Heads, Messrs. W. P. White and Co., the agents of the Blackwall line, placed themselves in communication with that vessel, and the wind being light, and from the eastward, charted the steam-tug *Lioness* and proceeded to the Heads.[24]

The weather was fine, with a slight southerly wind.

One reason for interest in the ship's arrival was that it carried the latest news from England and Europe. Another was its large cargo of hundreds of packages, cases, casks and barrels, and building materials including 262 slabs of stone, steps, sills and sinks. Most of the cargo consisted of consignments for merchants. When the *Norfolk* departed again for London on 31 March, it was carrying wool, sheep skins, tallow, copper, various packages of returned goods and 82 570 ounces [2.3 tonnes] of gold.[25] The ship would later take some of the first experimental cargoes of frozen carcasses from Melbourne to England.[26]

The passengers were reported to have 'enjoyed very good health during the passage ... and presented Captain Reynell and his officers with handsome testimonials, thanking them for their kindness and attention during the passage'.[27] In addition to his reference from Gravesend, John Langford was issued with a certificate of Discharge and Character, recording that 'his ability and conduct were good'. John was 40 and Harriet 36. Shipping records list the children as aged one, four, six, eight and 11. They were among thousands of immigrants arriving that summer.

2
The markets and Elizabeth Miller

Like Gravesend, Melbourne was a city by a river near the sea. Shipping played an important role in its economic life, with vessels constantly arriving from Europe, other Australian colonies and elsewhere. In terms of its population and culture, it was 'a Victorian community overseas.'[1] Laid out parallel to the river in a rectangular grid of wide streets, it had few buildings taller than two storeys. Unlike Gravesend, however, it was less than 25 years old and in a state of extreme flux.

When Victoria had separated from New South Wales in 1850, Melbourne was a rural township with a population of around 30 000. After a series of gold rushes in the colony, by 1858 its population increased to 140 000 and it was on a trajectory of growth that would make it Australia's largest city for the remainder of the century. Despite this, the colony's population was very decentralised, with less than a third living in the metropolis. A large proportion of the new population was transient, males outnumbering females.

The first elections for Victoria's new bicameral parliament were held in 1856. It was a struggle to provide the necessary amenities for the growing population, but the city was rapidly acquiring the symbols of progress. Gas had been connected in 1856, and the water supply had just come on tap in 1857. 'Sewerage was carried away in huge open gutters, at their worst in the centre of town',[2] with a comprehensive modern sewerage system still several decades away. Construction of the first suburban railways began in the 1850s. The edge of the built-up area extended into what is now North Melbourne, Collingwood, Richmond and South Melbourne. There was a new bluestone town hall, a Parliament House and a university, and a public library soon to open. A range of new industries had sprung up to service the needs of the new population. An air of the provisional was discernible from the unsealed roads, canvas verandahs and tent cities on the south side of the Yarra and in Royal Park.

The Langfords rented a cottage at 6 Guilford Lane, a narrow residential backstreet off Queen Street in the central city. The small stone building had two rooms, with a tiny shed at the back of the yard behind. It was in a neighbourhood of attached single- and double-storeyed brick shingled houses. In 1860, a majority of the children in Victoria aged 5-15 were receiving an education, and of these three-quarters were at church schools.[3] There were various Anglican schools around central Melbourne, and the three government schools within the city boundary were in theory open to all. No doubt the Langfords took advantage of this early education system.

John Langford found work as a fruiterer at the Eastern Markets. Also known as Paddy's markets, these had opened in 1847 between Bourke, Stephen (Exhibition) and Little Collins Streets to service the eastern side of town. At the time the existing Western Markets were frequently inaccessible on account of the marshy ground and deep gully along Elizabeth Street, where people occasionally drowned in floods during wet weather. Covered trading areas were constructed on the square site in 1859, these being verandah-fronted shops along the western side, with four parallel arcades numbered A-D consisting of timber pillars 14 feet high below twin arched roofs of corrugated zinc.[4] The area underneath was surfaced with flagstones. When first opened in May 1859 there were 224 stands, hired out by market gardeners, fruiterers and other dealers.[5]

All kinds of produce were sold there. It became known as the best place to buy vegetables: depending on the time of year, there were cabbages, carrots, Scotch kale, lettuces, leeks, onions, parsnips, potatoes, radishes, turnips, swedes, beets, celery, pumpkins, cucumbers, peas and beans for sale. One could also buy apples, melons, grapes, pears, plums and almonds, and bunches of mint, sage, thyme and water cress as well as cut flowers. Butter, eggs, rabbits, ducks geese, hens, turkeys and pigs were also available. Much of the produce came from distant parts of the state, and even interstate, arriving by train or boat or horse transport.

As John Langford was not a grower by experience or rural habitation, he would have served as an agent or dealer for producers. There are references to his 'persevering industry and hard labour'.[6] Trade was in direct competition between the many stallholders, with the relationship between growers and non-growers described in later years as hostile.[7] Daily life started before dawn.

Like all markets within the city boundaries, the Eastern Markets were controlled by the Melbourne City Council, whose regulations guided the trading. [8]

> The market was to commence by the ringing of a bell at 6.00 a.m. from September 1st to February 28th; at 8 a.m. during autumn and the winter months, and must close at sunset throughout the year. Out of hours trading before the bell ringing entailed a fine of ten shillings. A market inspector with assistants was required to preserve order and to prosecute any person creating a disturbance, also 'any person using gross or indecent language cursing or swearing in the market.' Other regulations provided for correct scales and similar fair dealing.[9]

View east across central Melbourne in 1860. The Langfords were living at the end of Guildford Lane (far left) at about the time this photograph was taken. The State Library is visible at centre distance, its portico not yet constructed. The first Melbourne Hospital is to the right of this, with spire of the newly completed Wesleyan Church rising behind.
SOURCE: STATE LIBRARY OF VICTORIA

Regulations stated that if a stallholder did not arrive within half an hour of opening time, the stall could be leased to someone else.[10] There were always more sellers than there were stalls, so stands would spill out into the street, and despite the arcades, traders were still exposed to the weather. While the markets were open six days per week, Wednesday and Saturday were the busiest days, when producers would travel in to sell wholesale. Adjacent streets would be littered with rubbish after trading days. Trade fluctuated with the seasons, and was busiest in the run up to Christmas. The area was sometimes used to hold public meetings.

The market took on a different character on Saturday nights, when it was open until 11 pm. The range of stalls broadened to include anything a household might need, selling by gaslight in 'a noisy jumble of shouting tradesmen, haggling customers, squealing animals and fervent political orators'.[11] A reporter from the *Melbourne Leader* visited one Saturday evening in the late 1850s.

> Here we have long lines of stalls, carts and wheelbarrows, selling everything. Any quantity of butter and cheese far removed from the dairy ... One man is sailing up and down, like Van Tromp, in the channel, with a broom aloft, proclaiming, 'brooms for a bob'. Another is presiding deftly over a heap of potatoes, which in the brogue of his country, he is striving to invest with an air of 'illigance'. Cheap John, in a cart ornamented with

The Eastern Market was a scene of constant activity. In this 1864 view across Bourke Street from the north-west Exhibition Street (then known as Stephen Street) is visible in the top left corner, with the Haymarket Hotel at right.
SOURCE: STATE LIBRARY OF VICTORIA

Chinese lanterns, and hung round with rifles, saddles and bridles, ladies' reticules, and bundles of clothes pegs, is busy selling a packet of envelopes, letter paper and sealing wax by Dutch auction. The greatest competition is in apples – we hear a man roaring at the top of his voice, 'heating happles, three pound a shilling'; another not less noisily, announces, 'bakers and bilers, four pounds to a shilling.' Next we come to a miniature drapery shop, where a man in a white beaver, with a blue paper of pins fastened round it, inviting attention to his wares. The feature of the markets is the confectioner' stalls, blazing with light, and glittering with wonderful feats in the art of making sugar candy: there are walking sticks of every kind, from bamboo to birch made in sugar, mutton chops and sheeps' heads that would deceive a butcher.[12]

In about 1864, the family moved to a small four-roomed timber house in Ridgeway Street off Little Collins, behind the Melbourne Club. Their house was on a block 25 by 54 feet on the eastern side of the street, where the Lyceum Club now stands. They lived there for the next 18 years. Their landlord was initially Mr R. Morris, then after 1867, Mr John Wombach. By this time the children were all teenagers.

Through their father the Langford children would have been introduced to the markets from an early age. If Harriet Langford didn't work on the stall with her husband, it was a walk of only half a city block west from Ridgeway Street to see him. Soon she could see her elder sons there too, as Robert began working as a fruiterer at age 17, Alfred having probably started there before him. James also later worked at city markets, first as a lessee then also as an inspector. The family developed a new circle of friends, which included another Kentish couple, the Pierces. James and Ellen Pierce had emigrated to Melbourne from Faversham, in 1855, and also had small children. James kept a tobacco shop in Elizabeth Street.[13]

In 1866, at age 17, Robert started working at the Fish Markets[14] which had just moved to a grand new building on the corner of Swanston and Flinders Street. Some trade, however, lingered on for a while in a small temporary timber building which had been set up next to the Princes Bridge in about 1864, and this is where Robert first started trading before soon moving across to the new market. Perhaps his father, the old Thames fisherman, had encouraged him to make the shift. He may have begun working there for an existing stallholder, opened a stall himself or been a hawker.

The new Fish Market building was like a squat ziggurat, three storeys high with a low roof and cast iron verandahs. (This was eventually replaced by the existing Flinders Street Railway Station in the 1900s.) A substantial proportion of the colony's wholesale fishing trade would pass through this building over the coming decades. Adjacent to the Yarra and Flinders Street Railway Station, it was supplied by boats docking along the river, freight trains and horse-drawn deliveries. The Melbourne City Corporation built and owned the complex, and operated it under a regime similar to the Eastern Markets. Melbourne City Council's Markets Committee oversaw its operation. Inside there was stall space for 12 fish wholesalers as well as railway offices, a newsagency, tobacconist and refreshment rooms. The trading areas were entirely enclosed. A shopper at the fish market could take home any kind of fish or crustacean, and game and poultry were also sold, including galahs and seagulls.

The character of Flinders Street at this time and its association with fish were determined by its closeness to the Yarra. The view looking west from Queen Street was flanked to the south by masts and rigging of ships approaching and leaving Queens Wharf, as well as a row of candelabra-like telegraph poles, while along the northern side of the street were the Customs House and various warehouses. The Princes Bridge Hotel had opened in the ground floor of a bluestone warehouse on the corner opposite the fish market in 1861. Seafood was sold on the street as well as in the market. Street vendors bought fish and oysters wholesale at the market in the early morning, then roamed nearby city blocks with their wheelbarrows and carts. Effluent from the fish market and from fish hawkers washing out their barrows collected in large open drains on either side of the street, the smell of which caused constant complaints to the Melbourne City Council.

As at the Eastern Markets, life was physically demanding. 'The Market opened every morning at 5 o'clock, and auction sales continue from that time to 8 o'clock and are resumed at 10 o'clock and continue until 11.30am'.[15] The early morning auctions were held by gaslight. Entering the building on a cold winter's morning, there would be a milling crowd of men in coats and hats, fishermen, hawkers and scruffy street urchins. Inspectors examined the fish prior to sale.

> Shortly after five o'clock the fish arrives in baskets, and is sold by auction by five salesmen, all of whom are vociferous at the same time in lauding the quality of the lots they offer for sale, and if 'chaff' of twenty or thirty loud voiced men, who take delight in making as much noise as possible, be added, we cannot be too far wrong in saying the scene is one of the liveliest.[16]

In summer, the most overwhelming sensation was the smell, which was apt to follow the worker home. The scene at the end of the day was of men with rolled-up shirtsleeves cleaning, sorting and bundling fish against a backdrop of carts, wooden crates, baskets and stalls.

Robert had learnt about running a business and playing the salesman while working with his father. Now he was striking out on his own. He had some 'very rough experiences in his struggles towards the goal of success'. While turnover could be very lucrative, fish salesmen tended to have a lower-class image, one writer of the time commenting, 'There is something about fish that has a not very elevating effect on the minds of those who deal in it.'[17] Another more snobbishly called the fish markets 'the social dung heap of Melbourne and suburbs'.[18] It was, however, a place where a shrewd businessman could prosper.

Robert sometimes travelled as a young man, on one trip getting lost in the Strathbogie Ranges for several days without food. He once admitted to having a fondness for drink, which may have begun when he, with his brothers and friends, stopped at one of the many nearby hotels after work. The same company might have supported his interest in sports, particularly football and cricket. He frequented Royal Park when young.

At some stage in the late 1860s, Robert became acquainted with William John Clarke, who later became Sir William Clarke, first Baronet of Rupertswood and the largest landowner in the colony after inheriting his father's estates. For many years when visiting Melbourne, Clarke's father, William John Turner Clarke, resided at the Port Phillip Club Hotel on the north side of Flinders Street, just across the road from the fish market. Robert talked about 'pleasant remembrances of associating with [Sir William] in the good old coursing days'.[19] Coursing was an English rural sport where greyhounds competed with each other to capture rabbits or hares. Sir William became President of the Victorian Coursing Club in the 1870s.[20]

While Robert Langford was not the eldest of his family, he was the first to wed, when soon after turning 23 in 1872, he married Elizabeth Miller.

~

Elizabeth's full name was Mary Elizabeth Lillian Miller, though she was also known as Elizabeth, or 'Lizzie' and Eliza to friends. Her father William Miller was originally from London. According to Elizabeth's sister Louise, he had first come out to Australia as a touring vaudevillian.

> He was a play plotter with Mr Brooks under engagement to Sir George Coppin, and both of them intended returning to England. My father, however, stopped in this country play plotting until Mr Brooks should return, but the above ship was wrecked and Mr Brooks drowned. My father then joined Mr Walter Scott (he later became Sir Walter Scott), and they did a good deal of acting in various places until the Gold Rush started and then changed their plans.[21]

If William Miller had worked in vaudeville in Melbourne during the early 1850s, he likely had some association with Coppin, an actor and entrepreneur who dominated the Melbourne entertainment industry from the 1850s onwards. Melbourne's vaudeville circuit was firmly established by this time,[22] providing one of the main forms of popular entertainment. Singers, comedians, dancers and actors would perform to audiences in theatres and other showhouses.

Coppin sometimes brought out famous singers and actors from Europe and America to tour Australia, including Gustavus Vaughan Brooke, a successful Irish actor for whom he twice arranged tours. The first was lengthy, lasting between February 1855 and May 1861.[23] The second was cut short before it began, when Brooke famously drowned with the sinking of the steamship *The London* in the Bay of Biscay in 1866.[24] William Miller was already in Victoria at the time of the first visit, having begun his second marriage with Mary Watson there in 1854.[25] [26] Brooke had toured the goldfields, and there he and Miller are more likely to have encountered each other because, like tens of thousands of others, Miller had left Melbourne for the goldfields in search of more lucrative possibilities.

Gold was discovered in Victoria in a long series of rushes beginning in 1851. Within a few years there were major finds in the Castlemaine, Bendigo, Ballarat and Maryborough districts. The Millers went to the goldfields outside Maryborough. A series of rushes had begun in the area in about 1855, with new finds continuing into the 1860s. The discovery of nuggets, such as one weighing 1050 ounces (29.77 kg) found in June 1855 and another of 1128 ounces (31.98 kg) found in 1856,[27] lured miners from across Australia and overseas. Tens of thousands of people might converge on a find within a month at a time when Melbourne itself had barely 100 000 people. They lived in makeshift camps, lacking in basic infrastructure. After the landscape had been churned over thoroughly, the bulk of the population moved on to the next find. They were gambling and few enjoyed spectacular success.

There was no rail link to the area, so gold diggers had to travel the 190 kilometres from Melbourne to Maryborough by horse or bullock transport. The goldfields were rough places. A Polish miner Seweryn Korzelinski described a typical scene at a camp near a new rush.

> On both sides tents, dotted here and there, up and down, under the trees and near the sheer cliffside, right and left, without symmetry of order, varying in shape. They form whitish blobs set in the surrounding panorama, as dictated by the needs, whims or fancy of their owners. In front of some tents fires, and near the fires men, all dressed alike. Round hats with wide brims, blue striped shirts, moleskin trousers, shoes or boots heavily soled with metal studs. Long beards indicate that either there is no time to take care about one's appearance, or that no one cares about it.[28]

Elizabeth Miller was born into this rough, chaotic environment in 1855. Her earliest years were spent in Dunolly, a tent town, whose transient population is estimated to have peaked as high as 50 000 at the height of the rush there.[29] The main street, Broadway, was lined with canvas and timber shops and was dusty or muddy depending on the season. The general stores sold essential items such as picks, shovels, cabbage tree hats, rope, axes, lanterns and camp ovens, and the opening of a new

Elizabeth Miller would have attended Carisbrook Common School No. 130. She is most likely present amongst the children in this 1866 snapshot of the school and its pupils. Headmaster Edwin Parnell is standing on the footpath in the front.
SOURCE: PHOTOGRAPH COURTESY DARYL MCGLEISH

An 1866 view of the newly finished St Paul's Anglican Church in Carisbrook where Robert and Elizabeth were married in August 1872.
SOURCE: PHOTOGRAPH COURTESY DARYL MCGLEISH

store was marked by the raising of a flag on a long pole. A return trip to Melbourne took 10 to 14 days, and hold-ups were not uncommon. Several entertainment venues soon opened in Dunolly, including Coleman's Rotunda Theatre, opened by a colleague of George Coppin. Here internationally famous companies and entertainers such as Gustavus Brooke would perform.

Elizabeth and her younger siblings were thus children of the goldfields. William ran a butcher's shop and marquee store at Dunolly for three years and tried some prospecting. Like other goldfield families, they would have lived in a tent or a small hut. Elizabeth's next sister Louise was born in a tent during a storm,[30] and over the following years further children, Agnes, Ernest, Samuel and Frederick, were born. They moved on to the nearby Talbot and the Marjorca goldfields, with the children moving between various makeshift schools set up at the tent town around each new find. Their daily lives must have been something of a struggle.

William and Mary Miller continued to search for gold, working on shallow claims, using a windlass to raise the soil in a bucket, then cradle and puddle machine to wash out the gold. 'The miner's main tool was a bar sharpened at both ends.' Deep shafts had to be lined with timber and the work was often dangerous, William once rescuing a Mr Lawrence from a collapsed shaft by digging him out with a penknife. According to Louise, her father 'lost all his money in mining'.[31]

Elizabeth was about 10 when in 1865 they moved to a farm at Harrison's Hill, around three kilometres outside the pretty town of Carisbrook. The town had a population of around 1000 and was only seven kilometres from Maryborough. Jules Verne described it in his 1867-68 travel story, *The Children of Captain Grant* (also known as *On the Track*), which he called 'Carlsbrook'.

> There was a bank, a town-hall, a market, a school, a church, and a hundred perfectly uniform brick houses, all built in a regular quadrilateral, crossed by parallel streets in the English fashion. Great activity reigned in the streets of Carlsbrook, a remarkable symptom in so young a town. It seems as if, in Australia, the towns grew like trees by the heat of the sun. Business men hurry along the streets, gold is carried along, escorted by the native police, to be sent away, coming from Bendigo or Mount Alexander.[32]

Although in a goldmining district, the main economic activity was agriculture. Initially, William continued prospecting 'working a wim claim close to home and near Woolbrook Gold Mine'.[33] What finally granted William a solid living were piles of bones on the district's farms, a valuable raw material for making fertiliser. He set up a bone grinding business supplying bone meal to local farmers, which proved much more successful than prospecting had been. He also secured the contract to deliver mail between Carisbrook and Maryborough. Eventually he came to own five houses and land around Carisbrook, and became an orchardist.[34]

The children divided their time between the town's state school and the farm. '[We] had to walk into Carisbrook school twice a day'.[35] The older children probably attended the Church of England School under the head teacher Edward Parnell. There were the usual chores of farm life. We 'had plenty to do before going and on returning home. There were cows to milk and horses and pigs to feed', and the cows had to be brought home every morning and night.[36] The children would sometimes go on long horse rides to Clunes, Talbot, Chinaman's Flat, Craigie, Marjorca and Maryborough.

Like her sister, Elizabeth would have left school in her early teens. Whether she was working in Maryborough when she met Robert Langford, or had moved to Melbourne, or whether Robert was visiting the district to see produce suppliers is not known, but they became interested in each other, and were married on 5 August 1872 at St Paul's, the small bluestone Anglican Church in Carisbrook. Elizabeth was 17.

3
The fish salesman

In December 1873, Robert wrote a letter to the Melbourne City Council Markets Committee requesting permission to conduct auction sales at the fish market; this was duly granted.[1] He was moving up the professional hierarchy. From 1874, he is listed in directories as an independent fish agent, then fish merchant, so was clearly working for himself. By this time he was operating a stall. He evidently had an entrepreneurial streak and wasn't afraid to stand up on a rostrum.

To get from the water to the dinner table, fish typically passed through a distribution process involving five stages of handling. These have been identified as (1) fisherman/grower, (2) transportation, (3) wholesaler/fishmarket, (4) provider/ retailer/ processor and (5) public/consumer.[2] Sometimes intermediate stages could be skipped, such as when fishermen chose to sell directly to the public. Typically tension existed between the fisherman and wholesalers, the fishermen often resenting the margins charged by the wholesalers, or feeling that they were not always selling stock for a maximum price. Robert's role was at stage (3), and involved liaising with those active at each of the other stages.

Commercial directories listed nine other traders at the fish markets in 1874, although there would have been more. John Lewis was the market lessee and inspector. Scottish-born William Mentiplay had also begun at the Fish Markets in 1866, and became an auctioneer there in April 1871. William Hanneysee was originally from Berkshire, and had commenced business at the market as a wholesale fishmonger and general auctioneer in 1872. Joseph Jenkins was a London-born fish salesman and auctioneer, who also had premises in Prahran. Other traders were Charles Palmer, commercial agent and auctioneer; Lewis Brooks, restaurant and fishmonger; Samuel Bowden, oyster salesman; and Thomas Harrison, oyster and fish salesman. Mrs Alitha Baker was one of the few female traders in an overwhelmingly male-dominated industry. She was the widow of fishmonger John Baker, and had taken over his business at 40 Swanston Street upon his death in 1869 and relocated it to the Fish

Late 19th century panoramic view showing the Fish Markets at centre with one of the entrances to the old Flinders Street Railway Station at left, with the Yarra River behind. The industrial character of South Melbourne is evident from the chimney stacks visible across the river.
SOURCE: ROYAL HISTORICAL SOCIETY OF VICTORIA

Market.[3] Although rivals, these people were also Robert's professional peers, and in many cases, personal friends. As well as auctioneers and stallholders, there were dozens of Chinese fish hawkers, who occupied a bay at the west end of the market. The Chinese had a strong presence in the industry.

For their first few married years, Robert and Elizabeth lived in West Melbourne, first in Stanley Street, then in Roden Street. They were close to their families, making occasional trips out to Carisbrook. John Langford continued working at the Eastern Markets.

In March 1873, Robert's older brother Alfred became ill. He was admitted to the Yarra Bend Asylum in Kew on 20 March, paralysed down one side, weakened, and barely able to walk or speak. He was slowly succumbing to brain disease. The family and a number of friends came in to see him several times a week, but his condition steadily worsened. He died on 17 May 1873, aged 26.[4]

The other Langford children were all adults by now, and in 1876 James Langford married a Miss Euphemia Rea. They named their first child Robert, after his uncle. Within a year of Elizabeth's wedding her 16-year-old sister Louise married miner Alexander Charles McDonald. Robert's sister Harriet later married a Swedish immigrant, Charles Johnson, in 1881.

James Langford also began working at the fish market, probably initially with Robert. In 1871 the Markets Committee had begun putting the operation of the

View of the 1865 Fish Market building on the corner of Swanston and Flinders Streets, taken in the 1890s. The building was demolished to make way for the existing Flinders Street Railway Station in the late 1900s.
SOURCE: ROYAL SOCIETY OF VICTORIA

markets out to tender, with competitive bidding for an annual lease. John Lewis had been lessee in 1871-73, followed by Robert Atkinson in 1874 and W. Lewis in 1875-78. James Langford tendered for the lease in April 1878, securing it with a bid of £1415 over John Lewis's bid of £1325.[5] On obtaining the lease, James also became Assistant Inspector of the Fish Markets, the appointment approved by the Markets Committee in April 1878.[6] Inspectors' range of duties included collecting dues, and generally supervising the smooth operation of the markets on behalf of the committee.

The following year Lewis took out the lease ahead of James with a tender of £1855.[7] James wrote to the Markets Committee in May 1879 requesting permission to act as a salesman and auctioneer at the markets, which was duly granted.[8]

In March 1882 Robert Langford wrote to the Market Committee requesting a permanent inspector be appointed at the Fish Market to replace the roles performed by the Inspector of General Markets and Assistant Inspector. He recommended John Lewis as a suitable candidate. The matter was referred to the Inspector of General Markets, asking for his views on whether the position was necessary and what an inspector's duties might be.[9] The colonial government was about to appoint an inspector to ensure that no undersized fish were sold in contravention of the *Fisheries Act*, and it was proposed to combine this role with that of Fish Market Inspector, the appointee's salary being paid by council and the government.[10] The office of Inspector of the Fish Market was duly created, with the Inspector of General

Markets, Mr McDonald, preparing a schedule of duties. Eligible candidates recommended to council in June 1882 were John Lewis, Henry Coulthis, D. C. Way and Joseph Gaffe.[11] John Lewis was duly appointed.

Having advocated the appointment of a permanent fish market inspector, a few years later the Langfords were embarrassed to find themselves being prosecuted by him. In 1883 one of the brothers was caught selling 'stinking fish' at the wharves. Fish agents were sometimes tempted to do this to generate some return for fisherman for stock that would otherwise be rejected at the fish markets. A letter requested attendance at a Market Committee meeting to discuss the charge, but no response or appearance were recorded.[12]

Robert submitted a claim to the Markets Committee early in 1880 for compensation for the cost of fish stolen at the market, but this was disallowed.[13] Another compensation claim for damage caused to stock by defective pipes at the market was referred to the lessee before being settled by the Town Clerk for £5.[14]

A reporter from the *North Melbourne Advertiser* visited the markets at sales time in 1883.

> There are five auctioneers conducting the sales, Messrs R. Langford and Co.; Ritchie and Co.; Paice and Mentiply, whose combined voices constitute a babel second only to the Flemington saddling paddock on Cup day. The lorries and wagons used in conveying the fish from the steamers and railway stations are driven into the building where they serve as an extempore rostrum from which the knights of the hammer conduct their business ... The cream of the market generally goes to the clubs and different hotels. I noticed wagon loads of fish and sacks of oysters which had just arrived by steamers, piled up alongside the different offices. Messrs R. Langford and Co., who have earned the reputation of being the premier salesmen, get through from 700 to 1,000 baskets weekly, and at one season of the year as many as 4,000 pairs of rabbits.[15]

By 1883 there had been a significant turnover in tenants at the Fish Markets since Robert had begun as an auctioneer. There began to be complaints that the building was too crowded. Commercial directories list nine traders at the Fish Market in that year, again not a comprehensive list: Thomas Paice, Mrs J. J. Baker, Croskell, Richie & Co, Lewis Brooks, Percy Jenkins, E. N. Phillips, William Mentiplay, Alexander Hall and Robert Langford. Thomas Paice was originally from Tasmania, and is listed as a fishmonger and game auctioneer at the markets from 1882. Croskell, Richie & Co were salesmen at the markets from about this year onwards, though had been operating as carriers since 1867. They also operated as general auctioneers, house and land agents. Percy Jenkins was a son of Joseph Jenkins, mentioned above.[16]

John Denton, although not listed at the Fish Market in directories, also had a wholesale fish business operating there. He had auction rooms at 244 Smith Street in Fitzroy, where he operated as an auctioneer, land and money agent, dividing his time between the Fish Markets at sales time in the morning and the auction-room activities in the afternoon.[17] The tendency for fish salesmen to also be involved in other auctioneering and sales activities, as exemplified by John Denton, was a common pattern, and reflected both the generic nature of sales and auctioneering skills, and the fact that the market's morning sales schedule allowed time for fish salesmen to pursue other activities later in the day. Other salesmen who diversified in this way included Croskell, Richie & Co, William Hanneysee and Joseph Hill.

Established at the fish markets, Robert's eye began roaming for other opportunities. He was an expert on the fishing industry, and fishmongering was the base profession from which he began to diversify from the early 1880s. Over the following years, he began buying property, and started conducting real estate and other general sales. His property purchases were not entirely speculative at first, such as the purchase of a house for his parents in Curran Street, Hotham, and another house he bought in Richmond, which was let out cheaply to Elizabeth's sister Louise.

As their businesses developed, Robert and James gradually took on employees. Auctioneers needed assistants, people to mind stalls, process stock and transport it. Thomas Paice was a long-term employee of Robert's. The Langfords' payroll also included relatives in need. Elizabeth Langford probably worked at the business, particularly in the early years. At one stage Elizabeth's sister Louise and brother-in-law, Alexander, were working for them.

Interior view of Swanston Street Fish Market at sales time. Signage for the Langford Brothers stall is visible at far right.
SOURCE: STATE LIBRARY OF VICTORIA

> We struggled along for a few years until my sister ... wrote and told my husband and I to come to Melbourne as her husband had a business in the Fish Market and would find work for us. He then took up a shop in Molesworth Street, North Melbourne, and put me into it, while my husband got a job in the Fish Market. We managed to make a living, but I had to work day and night cleaning hundreds of fish, frying and smoking daily, and stocking poultry and rabbits as well. I was only nineteen years of age and had four children to care for and tend as well as looking after the shop.[18]

Fisheries was one of the minor primary industries in Victoria. 'Although the average price of fish was 2d per pound, colonials were not a fish eating people.'[19] However, the trade was increasing, stimulated by the ongoing development of fisheries, improvements in transportation and the growing size of the Melbourne market. Subject fisheries gradually expanded from Port Phillip Bay only in the 1850s to cover Victorian and Bass Strait coastal zones, to interstate fisheries and eventually international sources such as South Africa and Europe.[20] Robert's business came to draw upon an Australasian network of suppliers, which was described in advertisements.

> Robert Langford & Co., General Auctioneers, Commission and Forwarding Agents, Fish, Game and Oyster Salesmen, Fish Markets Melbourne. Agents for - The Moreton Bay Oyster Co., Brisbane, Maryborough Oyster Co., Queensland; Gibbons Celebrated Oyster Fisheries, Sydney; Georges River Oyster Fisheries, Sydney; Sydney Prawn Co.; South Australia Fishing Co., Adelaide; Hobart and New Zealand Fisheries; and Fishing and Game Stations in the colony of Victoria. All consignments punctually attended to. Fish, game, oysteries etc. packed and forwarded to all parts of the colonies on the shortest notice.[21]

Maintaining this network required trips to the other colonial capitals, including Brisbane. Robert said he was once shipwrecked in New Zealand, which probably occurred on a business trip.

Robert was socially amiable, but evidently had the kind of commercial hard-headedness that is needed to build fortunes. While it is difficult to plot precisely the growing financial returns of Robert's various business activities, it is clear that he had become comfortably off by the mid-1880s. He rose from being the man behind the stall to a manager of employees, a man with servants. He was riding on the fishes' back and on the prosperity of the wider economy.

At a time in their lives when they were young and energetic, Robert and Elizabeth began to enjoy significant amounts of leisure time. Robert contemplated standing for Hotham Council.

4
The move to Curran Street

Robert and Elizabeth had moved to Hotham in about 1877, where they rented an eight roomed house at the southern end of Dryburgh Street before shifting to Chapman Street. They were to live in the area for nearly 10 years.

Hotham

Hotham was still a young suburb, in 1879 less than 40 years old and occupying land which only a lifetime earlier belonged to the Wurundjeri (or Woiworung) tribe.[1] Aboriginals are believed to have previously occupied south-eastern Australia for at least 40 000 years, which is before the first humans arrived in the Americas.[2] Consisting of seven clans, the Wurundjeri tribal territory stretched from Port Phillip Bay west to Daylesford and Broadford and east to Jamieson and Moe. Smallpox epidemics are estimated to have halved their 1788 population by 1835, the disease having spread to the region by 1803.[3] They called the area, now occupied by Royal Park and Parkville, Doutta Galla and had camps there as late as 1843.[4] Few physical traces of their presence remain around North Melbourne.

Melbourne itself had been informally established in 1835 and recognised by the colonial government of New South Wales the following year.[5] A town reserve of three miles by one mile was laid out, to which North Melbourne was added in 1840. According to Hoddle, North Melbourne in 1841 was 'a collection of buildings erected without any definite plan upon suburban allotments'.[6] In as far as the suburb existed in the 1840s, it was an accidental scattering of buildings over the northern edge of the city grid. Its residents would have seen the bonfires lit on Flagstaff Hill to celebrate the secession of the colony of Victoria from New South Wales in 1850. In that year construction of a Benevolent Asylum began in bushland at the western end of Victoria Street, its massive edifice becoming the suburb's dominant landmark of the

View of the north side of Hotham in the early 1870s. The large building on the hillside to the right is the Benevolent Asylum, a prominent North Melbourne landmark demolished in 1911. The double-spires at far left belong to the Wesleyan Church, demolished 1936.
SOURCE: NORTH MELBOURNE LIBRARY

19th century. A gold rush immigrant, Albert Mattingley, still wrote in 1852 of the suburb's 'beautiful park-like appearance', it being 'richly carpeted with grass and noble red gum trees, where Aboriginal tribes still occasionally camped'.

In the early years the suburb was referred to as North Melbourne, but was renamed after the second Victorian Governor, Sir Charles Hotham, when the municipality of Hotham was declared in 1859. John Davis was elected mayor of the first

council in that year. In 1862 there were 1500 ratepayers, contributing to a total revenue of £2400.[7] It became Borough of Hotham in 1863, then the town of Hotham. Land subdivision moved progressively in a north-west direction, the subdivided areas soon covered with tents, cheap housing, stables, corrugated iron sheds and hotels. There were 1740 dwellings in the suburb by 1861. The Melbourne Gas Company had installed pipes in North Melbourne by 1859, with connection to the Yan Yean water supply occurring in the mid-1860s. The trees were cleared, the swamps were filled and a cover of buildings ensued.[8]

By 1877 Hotham's fortunes were rising. Civic ambition was conspicuous in the grand new Town Hall on the corner of Errol and Queensberry Streets, which was finished in 1876. A competition was won by architect George Raymond Johnson, with a design which included a court house, post office and a five-storey clock tower at the corner. The commercial strip along Errol Street was like the self-contained main street of a country town, only a mile from Melbourne's GPO. The most substantial landmark was the Benevolent Asylum, a massive neo-Gothic edifice set amongst spacious gardens at the western end of Victoria Street. Surrounding it was housing stock which varied greatly in quality, more working than middle-class. There were streets of comfortable detached villas and ornate terraces, but larger numbers of workmen's shabby timber cottages. There were no underground sewers, with backyard privies serviced by contractors from back lanes. In addition to innumerable small workshops, there was a lot of heavy industry; there were ironworks and other large factories producing agricultural implements, boots and clothing.

On 4 September 1879, Robert attended an auction where he purchased a corner block of land on the west side of Dryburgh Street and south side of Curran Street, in Hotham. He took out a mortgage to pay for it, which he settled on 7 December 1882.[9]

Curran Street

Curran Street and that section of Dryburgh Street had been laid out about 20 years earlier.[10] Both streets were 1.5 chains wide (1 chain = 20 metres), consistent with the standard subdivision street width established by Robert Hoddle and used elsewhere in North Melbourne and around the state. The exact source of the street's name, Curran, is uncertain. There were several early Melbourne settlers with that name. In a discussion of street names in Hotham the journalist Edmund Finn ('Garryowen') wrote 'there we have quite an extensive commingling of English, Irish, Scotch and Colonial worthies. We have streets named after Peel, Erskine, O'Connell, Shiel, Curran ...',[11] suggesting the reference may be to John Philpot Curran (1750-1817), an Irish lawyer, statesman and advocate of Catholic rights.[12]

The land along Dryburgh Street north of Erskine Street was subdivided into Sections 85, 96, 87, 88 and 89 of the Parish of Jika-Jika, in the County of Bourke. That general area was known as Hotham Hill. The original Crown subdivision of the land between Curran Street and Flemington Road included the creation of Little Curran Street, a laneway giving access to the rear of the Allotments in Section 87. This originally gave access from Melrose Street through to the eastern end of Curran Street. As further subdivisions occurred, two smaller lanes branching from Little Curran Street were also created, these being Curran Lane and Piers Lane.

Land fronting Curran Street was sold by the colonial government as Allotments 1-12 of Section 88 and 12-22 of Section 87 in three sales by auctioneers Gemmel, McCaul and Co. The first at midday 6 September 1865 was scheduled to sell all blocks in Section 87, though along Curran Street only Allotments 13 and 14 passed.[13] At the next sales at 2 pm on 26 August 1867, Allotments 10-12 along Curran Street were sold.[14] The remaining Allotments 3-9 in Section 88 and 13-22 in Section 88 were auctioned at 2 pm 15 October the same year.[15] (Allotments 1 and 2 were granted to the Roman Catholic Church.) The upset price at each sale was £150 per acre.

The first house was built along the street in 1868 at what is now 1 Curran Street. It was situated on the larger Allotment 10 of Section 88, which had been sold to a farmer, Patrick Reilly, at the Land Sale of 1867. The new five-roomed brick dwelling was built on the eastern side of the site the following year, the allotment later being subdivided into two properties and a house built on the western site in 1884/85. By 1869, there had been two additional timber houses built along the street on parts of subdivided Allotments 14 and 17, with two brick houses being erected in the street during or about 1870.[16]

By the time Langford bought the site for his new house in 1879, Curran Street had developed into a busy neighbourhood. Subdivisions had brought the number of rateable properties along Curran Street to 34, from an initial Crown subdivision of 22. There were 25 dwellings spread about equally between each side of the street. Of these 12 were brick and the remainder timber, with most containing three or four rooms. Only seven of the 25 houses were not owner occupied. Occupations represented by the street's residents were contractor, civil servant, bookbinder, carter (5), gardener, wheelwright, labourer (4), painter (4), constable, stonemason, carrier, traveller, carpenter, and barman. Most people living in the street had British surnames.[17]

View looking west along Queensberry Street, Hotham, from the intersection with Howard Street in c.1870, prior to the construction of the existing Town Hall.

SOURCE: STATE LIBRARY OF NEW SOUTH WALES, MITCHELL LIBRARY

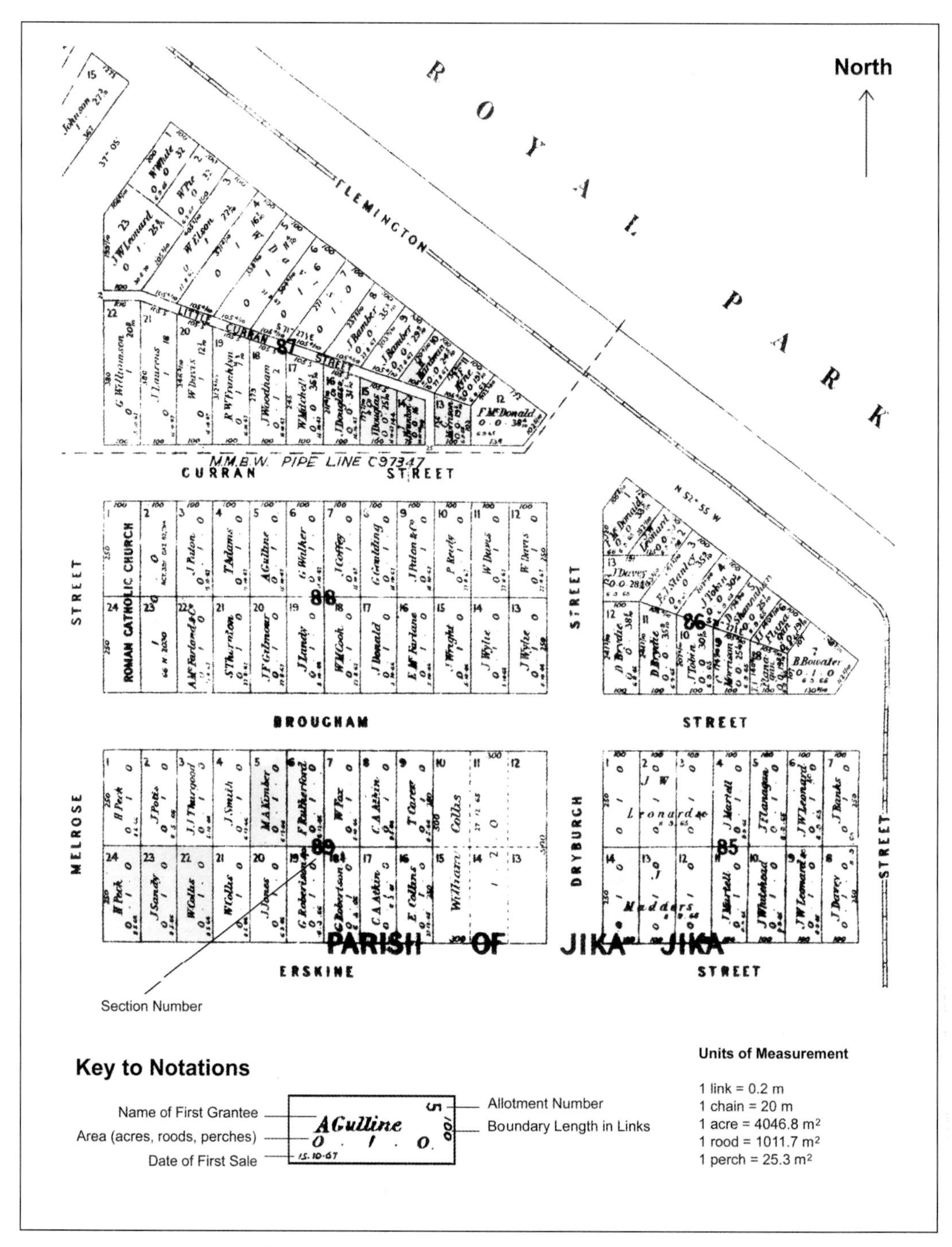

Parish plan showing the original subdivision of Hotham Hill. Allotments 11 and 12 on the corner of Curran and Dryburgh Streets in section 88 were originally sold to William Davis. SOURCE: LAND VICTORIA, CROWN (STATE OF VICTORIA), 2004. ALL RIGHTS RESERVED.

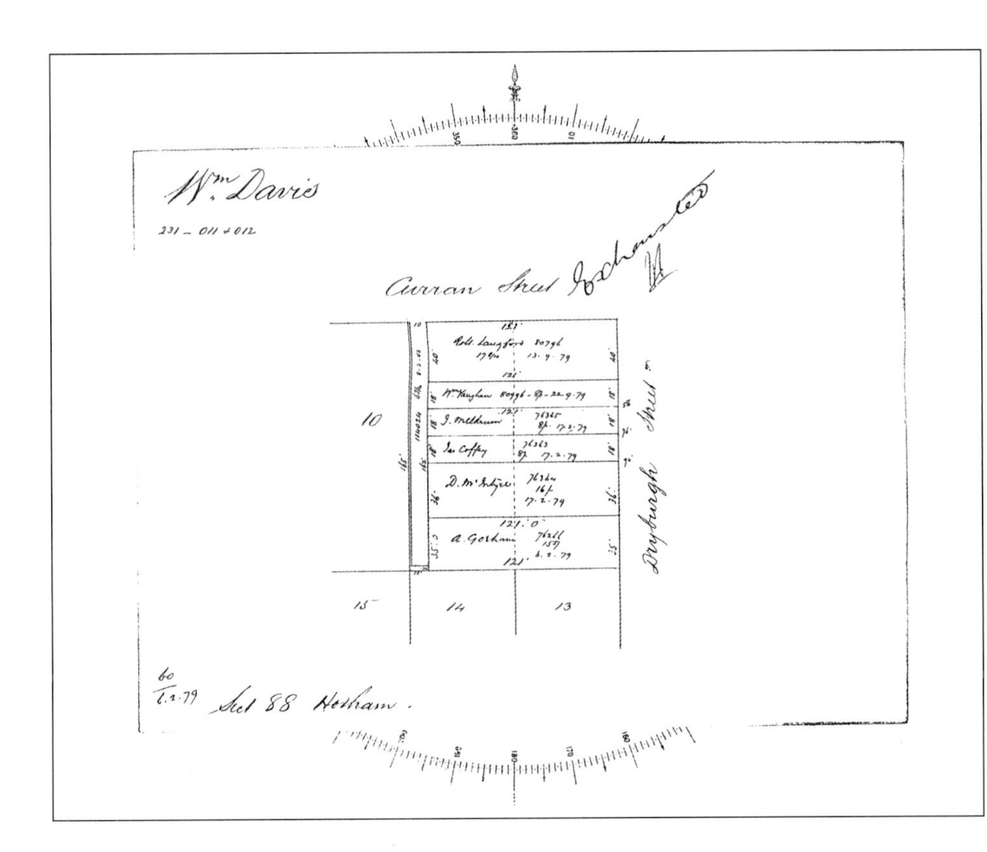

Plan showing the subdivision by William Davis of the combined Allotments 11 and 12 into a series of smaller sites with frontages onto Dryburgh Street in 1879. Robert Langford purchased the northern site on the corner with Curran Street.

Writing in the 1880s, 'Garryowen' commented on the development of the area.

> When a large portion of Carlton and Hotham was put into the market, numbers of people who had saved money from the early gold years (and better still, knew how to keep it), invested it there to advantage ... The present exceptionally superior appearance of those suburbs, as compared with other localities, may be attributed to the relatively late period when the greater part of the land was sold, and the judgement envinced by the land speculators in subdividing their purchases.[18]

The block Robert Langford purchased had been part of Allotments 11 and 12, which were sold for £220 to William Davis of Carlton at the second sales in 1867. The 1868 Hotham Rate Books describe the properties as two pieces of wasteland, each worth £100. Davis owned the two allotments until 1879 when their titles were combined and the land subdivided and sold in narrow allotments with frontage onto Dryburgh Street. The resultant blocks of land were initially without any formal street numbers, the first numbering in Curran Street and the northern end of Dryburgh Street not appearing in rate books or directories until 1888/89. Davis's subdivision included the creation of a new 10-feet wide laneway giving rear access to each of the new blocks.

Langford's block was on the corner, with a long frontage onto Curran Street, also facing onto Curran Street. This block has ever since maintained the boundaries of this time. Subsequent subdivision of adjacent Allotments 13 and 14 saw the extension of the rear laneway to Brougham Street.

The blocks along Curran Street and the north end of Dryburgh Street were not assigned street numbers until c.1889. Langford's block became 285 Dryburgh Street, later being renumbered 519 Dryburgh Street in 1917.[19]

The neighbourhood

The site of Langford's block overlooked Dryburgh Street to the east, Curran Street to the north and Royal Park to the north-east across Flemington Road and the intersection of these streets.

Royal Park had been proposed as a place for public recreation and amusement as early as 1844, when a Melbourne Corporation Committee submitted a petition to the Governor and the Colonial Secretary. Final approval was eventually given in 1854 for a reserve of 283 hectares to be put aside, its southern boundary defined by Flemington Road.[20] In its native condition the area was open grassland, lightly timbered, with tree species including red gum, yellow box, manna gum, messgate and peppermint. For many years sheep, cows and horses grazed on the thick cover of grass and travellers camped there, particularly during the gold rush years. It was from Royal Park that Burke and Wills set off on their ill-fated expedition into the interior of Australia in 1860. Melbourne Zoo was established on a central 20-hectare site in 1862.[21] Victoria's first elephant arrived there in 1875.[22] Paths were soon added linking the Zoo with Flemington Road, including one opposite Dryburgh Street. Various roads, sporting and maintenance facilities as well as plantings of exotic trees were later established in the park, but the essential character of the original bushland remains.

Flemington Road was one of the earliest to radiate out from Melbourne's city grid. It appears in a parish map of 1840, forking past the Moonee Ponds Creek to become the Mount Macedon and Upper Werribee Roads. In 1851 a bridge was finally built across the creek and approval was also given to widen Flemington Road to 99 feet (30.175 metres) by removing obstructing timber.[23] It was later further widened to 196 feet (60 metres). During the 1850s it was busy with traffic leaving for the Ballarat goldfields, and depending on the season, could be dusty or very boggy. Until 1877 Flemington Road had included a tollgate. Through the 19th century there were rough hills and embankments along the northern side of the road, which were still being levelled out early in this century.[24] Avenues of trees had been planted along both sides of the road by 1895. Through the 19th century and beyond, large herds of livestock would be driven down Flemington Road on their way to the Flemington Markets.

Moving to Curran Street

The North Melbourne Rate books, which described Davis's land as vacant during his years of ownership, mention a 'brick dwelling under construction' on Robert Langford's land in 1879/80. Robert and Elizabeth's new-six roomed brick house was valued at £60 by the following year when they had moved in. The five other allotments along Dryburgh Street in Davis's subdivision were sold to William Vaughan, J. Meldrum, James Coffey, D. McIntyre and R. Gosham. All of these had buildings on them by the end of 1879, with Vaughan building a four-roomed brick dwelling on the block adjacent to Langford's, this being initially valued at £20.[25]

In about 1881 Robert bought his parents a small cottage around the corner at what is now 13 Curran Street. This was on a large block comprising what had originally been Allotment 7 of the original crown subdivision. Robert built stables for himself at the rear. John Langford had decided to retire, possibly prompted by the closure of the Eastern Markets for rebuilding in 1879. Thinking of Kent, John and Harriet called their new home 'Milton Cottage'.

5
Councillor Langford

Melbourne's inner and outer suburbs were governed by a patchwork of municipal bodies. These were the lower strata of two tiers of government administering the Colony of Victoria. The upper level was the bicameral Victorian Parliament modelled on the British Houses of Parliament, consisting of the upper Legislative Council, which in 1883 had 30 members, and the lower Legislative Assembly which had 86 members.[1] Parliament dealt with all matters of importance colony wide. A Federal Council addressing 'matters of common Australasian interest' was to hold the first of a series of sessions on 25 January 1886; these ultimately led to the formation of a third federal tier of government in 1901.[2]

Municipal councils were created by the colonial government to deal with matters of primarily local concern. They were empowered to levy rates, and received subsidies from the Victorian government. Their role was to make, maintain, and control all streets, roads, bridges, ferries, culverts, watercourses and jetties within their boundaries. They were entrusted to regulate under proper by-laws the markets, pounds, abattoirs, baths, places of sewerage, lighting, water supply, fire prevention, and noxious trades. The wealthier suburbs vied with each other to build grandiose town halls, post offices and libraries. Many of the issues of concern to local residents were beyond the direct powers of the council, favourable outcomes requiring cooperation with adjoining municipal councils, the colonial legislature or private industry. Effective local councillors were adept lobbyists.

Hotham Council served an area of 17 800 residents and had an annual revenue of £14 000 drawn largely from local rates, publicans' licences and government subsidies.[3] There were nine serving councillors evenly distributed between the eastern, middle and western wards, each serving a standard three-year term. There was a paid staff of administrative officers, who occupied rooms on the ground floor of the Town Hall along Queensberry Street and in the Post and Telegraph Offices along Errol Street. Charles Randall was the Town Clerk and Treasurer, Charles Hill the

Hotham Town Hall where Robert attended fortnightly council meetings and functions after his election to Hotham Council in August 1882. This photograph dates from the late 1870s before the installation of the tower clock and the construction of the library at the right. SOURCE: STATE LIBRARY OF VICTORIA.

Surveyor, James Kearney the Rate Collector, J. Paton, Inspector of Dogs, Thistles and Collector of Statistics and J. MacGibbon, the Postmaster.

Robert Langford first contested a seat in 1881 and was defeated by 43 votes. The *Advertiser* cynically suggested: 'At present, the only assistance some men need to enter and take a seat at the council table is friendship.'[4] It did help an aspiring candidate to have friends who were serving councillors, publicans, and established campaign organisers. Publicans in particular could provide venues for campaign meetings and rallies. For aspiring candidates the first campaign is always the most difficult. On the other hand, there was usually only a limited field of candidates with the ability, motivation and spare time to assume what was an unpaid three-year obligation.

When an 'extraordinary vacancy' arose with the sudden resignation of Thomas Amott early in May 1882, over 100 ratepayers petitioned for Robert to stand again. In a letter to ratepayers he wrote: 'I consent with pleasure to stand for the Middle Ward, and if elected shall do all in my power to forward the interests of the town of Hotham.'[5] The three other candidates were Thomas Pilkington, Barnette Ellis and John Barwise. The poll was on Thursday 1 June after a busy week of electioneering. Ellis and Barwise addressed gatherings at Errol Street the previous Friday evening. Langford spoke to a crowd at the Courthouse Hotel on Monday. Auctioneering had made him accustomed to public speaking.

> There being no 'burning' question, on which the fate of a candidate depended, the contest partook more a friendly character ... Messrs Pilkington and Langford had a large number of cabs employed and the town was thoroughly canvassed ... About 6.30 p.m., the returning officer, together with the candidates, appeared on the small balcony on the Queensberry Street entrance. There was a very large number of electors present.[6]

The results were read out – Pilkington 280, Langford 239, Barwise 132 and Ellis 50. Coming in a close second, Robert said 'though beaten he was not discouraged'.[7] A second opportunity was not far away on the horizon.

A dinner was held on 9 June at the Melrose Hotel. Organised by Joseph Green, John Leadbeater and other friends, it was attended by most sitting Hotham councillors. Cr Green praised Robert, and hoped he would occupy a seat on the Town Council in the near future. He responded, 'It would always be his aim to do all in his power to advance the interests of the locality in which he resided' and that he would 'devote his time and talents to their [the ratepayer's] advantage'. Walkley's three-year term in the Middle Ward was coming to an end, with an election due in early August. He 'was not afraid of opposition, and in August he would come before the electors, and from his past conduct, he was not at all dubious about the result'. After the speeches, there were recitations and some singing.[8]

The abrupt retirement of the Hotham Mayor Thomas McInerney after he became insolvent led to another 'extraordinary vacancy' in Hotham's Western Ward, to be contested on 4 August. Robert initially stood again in that ward, where his rival was the implement manufacturer Hugh Lennon,[9] but then decided to contest the Middle Ward against Walkley instead.

On Thursday 27 July the campaign committee held a meeting at the Town Hall Hotel.

> There was a large attendance, and the following gentlemen agreed to canvass on Mr Langford's behalf. Messrs Stevens, Waddick, Gibbins, Champion, Lindsay, Wright, O'Callaghan, Downie, Evans, Henderson, Kennedy, McGrath, McCarthy, Hudson, Lee, McPherson, Smith. Mr J. Henderson was appointed chairman, and Messrs Power and Hudson joint secretaries.[10]

The ward was divided into areas for systematic canvassing. Walkely's campaign followed a similar program, both men giving a final campaign speech several days before the poll.

Robert's father-in-law, William Miller, had also become interested in local politics, and he stood for Carisbrook Council at around the same time. Perhaps he and Robert encouraged each other. The candidates all gave a campaign speech at a special rally the week before voting. William was particularly concerned with the condition of public thoroughfares.

> Mr Miller, a new candidate, in presenting himself for approval, found no fault with the administration of the present councillors, but remarked that for years the roads had been shamefully neglected. He described himself as 'Quality Jack', one that intended going in for all ratepayers having a fair benefit from the revenue of the borough, and for the improvement of the main roads, back streets, footpaths and gutters.[11]

Election day for Robert and William came in the second week of August. The elections held across Melbourne during this month were noted for their generally subdued conduct.

> The only contest was in the Middle Ward [Hotham], between Cr. Walkley and Mr Robert Langford. The committees of both gentlemen worked with zeal, and during the day a vast amount of hard canvassing was done. Every elector who could be reached was driven to the polling booth, and by four p.m. nearly 800 votes had been recorded. There was nothing left undone that could be done, and both gentlemen clearly saw that the fight was to be close and exciting. The cabmen had not much rest during the day, and from 9 a.m. till 5 p.m. the officers were kept fairly engaged. During the close of the poll, a large crowd congregated around the Town Hall, and after sitting patiently till 6.30 p.m., they were relieved from further anxiety by the Returning Officer declaring the state of the poll to be as follows :- Langford 535, Walkley 243, Majority for Langford 293.[12]

There were five candidates running for three seats in Carisbrook. William came second place with 106 votes, enough to secure a place.[13]

For Robert, at age 33, it was the beginning of a long career in local politics.

Hotham Council meetings were held every second Monday evening in the Town Hall in the council rooms on the first floor. The chamber was decorated in the 'modern Italian style', painted in 'shades of drab grey, quaker green, pink, lilac, cream etc.'[14] and opened onto a balcony overlooking Errol Street. 'Over the canopy of the Mayoral chair there [was] painted in the cove in relief ... a silver medallion of Her Majesty the Queen on a bronze ground, hanging from an ornamental tablet of grey and Cararra marble.' The Mayor's reception room was 'done more plainly, being in sombre tints and hues, such as quaker drabs, drab greens, buffs, and Tuscan reds'.[15]

Another large room on the first floor overlooking Queensberry Street to the north initially housed the library, but soon became used as a supper room. The Glaswegian chimes in the clock tower would sometimes sound erratically overhead.

The first meeting Robert attended was on 28 August. An advantage of being a councillor was that one could make connections with influential people in government and business. Councillors were typically successful businessmen, often with diverse commercial interests. Sitting around the table at the first meeting were Hugh Lennon, Joseph Green and John Laurens representing the Western Ward, Thomas Pilkington and Thomas Fogarty with Robert in the Middle Ward, and Thomas Henderson and William Reynolds from the Eastern Ward. (James Carroll was absent.) Laurens was a former grocer who was first elected to council in 1870 and a member of the Legislative Assembly after his election on a protectionist platform in 1877. Lennon and Henderson were manufacturers of agricultural implements. Fogarty was a wine and spirit merchant and had just been elected Mayor after the retirement of J. McInerney. Reynolds was a salesman at the local Meat Markets in Courtney Street.

The meeting began with the usual review of correspondence. A tender was accepted to lay 2000 cubic yards of crushed metal on Flemington Road. The appointment of a Goat and Dog Inspector was confirmed. The Hotham Literary and Debating Association was granted the use of the Inspector of Weights and Measures offices on the ground floor each Tuesday night for three months. The meeting was unusually brief because a Mayoral dinner was held afterwards in the upstairs supper room. Around 80 attended, including councillors from other suburbs and the Mayors of Fitzroy and Flemington.[16]

The need for a Goat Inspector was necessary in light of the large numbers of stray goats wandering though the suburb. An irate resident wrote to the *Advertiser* complaining about their numbers around Hotham Hill.

> I very often on a morning count as many as fifty together in some of the streets ... A large number of the residents of this district have gone to a great amount of trouble and expense in beautifying their places, in planting trees and shrubs in their small gardens, and all their labour and money are thrown away by these pests.[17]

Meanwhile, William Miller attended his first meeting of the new Carisbrook Council. When an agenda item concerned the stocking of a new artificial lake with fish, William sought Robert's advice.

> Cr Miller tabled a letter which he had received from his son-in-law ... The writer did not think that Gippsland fish would live in fresh water, but if the Council were satisfied to try them, he could get some from the Gippsland Lakes. If not, the best man to get a supply of live fresh fish from would be Mr Sam Morgan, of Ballarat West.[18]

In Hotham, beyond the mundane day-to-day tasks of administration there loomed larger issues of varying magnitude and urgency. One perennial issue was the North Melbourne Swamp. This was a large lagoon on the south-western outskirts of the suburb, which had become a dumping ground for rubbish and sewerage sludge. Representations were being made in August 1882 to the Department of Public Works to drain the swamp and begin a massive program of land reclamation.[19] Some work had begun at the end of 1882, but the area remained partial wasteland for some years.

In June 1882 Flemington and Hotham Councillors had sought funding to drain the Moonee Ponds Creek.[20] The creek was an unsightly watercourse along the western side of the Hotham town boundary, and the proposed works would enhance land values and encourage development along that side of the town. Approval was given in September 1882 to fill an area of stagnant land west of Buncle and Sutton Streets,[21] though the creek remained in poor condition. Other proposed works in the area included improving the nearby Hotham Cricket and Football Clubs Recreational Reserve. Cr Langford attended a meeting between Hotham and Flemington Councillors in November 1882 to discuss the immediate construction of a bridge across the creek at Barwise Street (now Racecourse Road).

There were regular calls to move the Benevolent Asylum to another suburb. It was argued that the inmates' interests would be better served if the valuable site was sold and the Asylum relocated to one more spacious on the suburban fringe. It was regarded by some as an overcrowded fire hazard. The matter would not be resolved until 1911.

Another issue was sanitation. Melbourne in the early 1880s had abnormally high mortality rates from infectious diseases when compared to British cities of a similar size. One reason was the lack of an effective, city-wide sewage disposal system. Construction of an underground sewer was first suggested in the late 1840s, but progress was held up for decades by political indecisiveness, with municipal councils unable to agree on the powers of the proposed new Board of Works to operate the system. Melbourne Town Clerk Edmund Fitzgibbon was the Board's leading advocate, and he periodically attended Hotham Council functions during the 1880s. *The Melbourne and Metropolitan Board of Works Act* was finally passed in 1890, with work commencing on the new sewerage system the following year.[22]

The introduction of trams had become contentious in Melbourne's inner suburbs in the early 1880s. Although opinion was divided, Hotham Council supported Parliament's proposed Tramways Bill, noting that unlike the existing omnibus services, the private operator proposed under the bill would pay tax. Robert had conservatively spoken against trams at an anti-tramway meeting while campaigning, agreeing the suburb was adequately served by its 120 cabmen, the proposed service

The foundation stone-laying ceremony for the North Melbourne Library, 22 January 1883. This was among the first of many official functions Robert would have attended as a councillor.
SOURCE: NORTH MELBOURNE LIBRARY.

was monopolistic, detrimental to local shopkeepers and was potentially dangerous.[23] The Tramways Act was nevertheless passed in 1884, with regular services through Hotham beginning soon after.

These and other issues were kept alive by the scrutiny of the local press, the election speeches of hopeful candidates and in letters to council from ratepayers. The leading local newspaper was the *North Melbourne Advertiser.* Issued each Friday, it was a four-page broadsheet costing one penny. Regular reporting included political news, social events and sports. Electoral opinion could be prompted by occasional savage editorials and letters to the editor. Robert started taking out extensive paid advertisements for his businesses, which may have helped his generally friendly relationship with the paper.

Robert was one of the less outspoken councillors during meetings. Between August 1882 and August 1884 he and Cr Reynolds had the lowest rate of attendance of the 62 regular and special council meetings held, being present at just over half of these meetings. (Crs Lennon and Pilkington missed no more than three meetings each over the same period.) Some of Robert's absences were due to business trips, such as in October 1882 when he applied for one month's leave to attend to affairs in Sydney and Brisbane.[24] The Public Works Committee held meetings every second Tuesday, and his presence at these compares more favourably. The Committee oversaw regular maintenance such as the repair of roads, fences, drainage and culverts and the tarring of footpaths, and as well as the construction and maintenance of municipal buildings. Robert seems to have been good at administration.

Official functions were an opportunity to mingle with influential people, and enjoy a little extravagance. Council had approved the outlay of around £5000[25] for the construction of a new library next to the Town Hall complex along Errol Street. The ceremony to lay the foundation stone was held on 22 January, 1883. Official guests included the Minister for Railways, several members of Parliament and the Mayors of Collingwood, Fitzroy and Brunswick. Robert and Elizabeth were in the official party. A large crowd of the interested public had gathered to watch. Soon after 1 pm the Mayor's wife, Mrs Fogarty, was escorted to the building site in her finery, and presented with a silver trowel by the council architect, George R. Johnson.[26] The mortar was smoothed and a massive block inscribed with gold lettering was lowered into place. Guests were served a luncheon in the Town Hall afterwards.

As he immersed himself in council affairs, Robert became more involved in other community activities. He was very interested in sport, notably football and cricket. Several local cricket clubs were formed in the early 1880s. He became a patron of the Hotham Hill, North Star and Queensberry Cricket Clubs, and Vice-President of the Crescent Cricket Club.[27] (Several other councillors were also cricket club patrons.) In December 1883 he presented a silver competition cup to the Hotham and West Melbourne Junior Cricket Clubs for use in competitions, which became known as 'the Langford Cup'.

Robert was also developing links with the Gippsland Lakes, in particular the fishing settlement of Paynesville. His association with the area would have begun through dealings with local fishermen. Situated on a small peninsula between Lake King and Lake Victoria with its eastern coast sheltered by nearby Raymond Island, the township lies about 260 kilometres east of Melbourne. The area had been wilderness until large-scale fishing began in the surrounding lakes in 1878. Fishermen began settling along the southern waterfront, the settlement initially becoming known as the township of Toonalook.

112 ADVERTISEMENTS.

Excelsior Auction Rooms,

71 QUEENSBERRY STREET. HOTHAM.

ROBERT LANGFORD & CO.,

GENERAL AUCTIONEERS.

House, Land, & Estate Agents.

FIRE & LIFE INSURANCE EFFECTED.

RENTS COLLECTED.

Agents for

ROYAL FIRE INSURANCE COMPANY,

MUTUAL LIFE ASSURANCE SOCIETY OF VICTORIA.

ROBERT LANGFORD & CO.,

General Auctioneers.

COMMISSION & FORWARDING AGENTS,

Fish, Game & Oyster Salesmen,

FISH MARKET, MELBOURNE.

Agents for

The Moreton Bay Oyster Co., Brisbane; Maryborough Oyster Co., Queensland; Gibbin's Celebrated Oyster Fisheries, Sydney; George's River Oyster Fisheries, Sydney; Sydney Prawn Co.; South Australian Fishing Co., Adelaide; Hobart and New Zealand Fisheries; All Fishing and Game Stations in the Colony of Victoria.

ALL CONSIGNMENTS PUNCTUALLY ATTENDED TO.

Fish, Game, Oysters, etc., packed and forwarded to all parts of the Colonies on the shortest notice.

Advertisement for Robert Langford & Co.
SOURCE: SANDS & MCDOUGALL DIRECTORY.

Every Easter Robert would travel across to Paynesville for the annual Regatta, to which he donated a cup. There he was known as 'Gubnor' Langford, and it was said that the Aboriginal community would greet him with a special corroboree. The race was a major town event. It was a 'picturesque site to watch [the boats] from the high bank as they scudded along the tranquil sheet of water in the lake below ... [Mr Langford] superintends the race, creates all sorts of amusements for young and old, he sets youngsters jumping and old buffers jigging and all sorts of sports, and puts his hand most generously in his pocket to give them liberal prizes all around.' Afterwards he would host a fishermen's banquet, during which his 50 guinea cup would be presented to the winner.[28]

Robert and Elizabeth were of Anglican background, but their religious enthusiasms wandered. In April 1884 Robert convened a meeting to help arrange the opening of a Hotham branch of the Bible Christian Church, a branch of the Methodist Church. Elected as chair, he promised to subsidise the cost of hiring a hall for the next meeting. The Church was an advocate for the Blue Ribbon temperance movement, of which Robert was a vigorous public supporter. 'He had known what it was to have an appetite for liquor, and had signed the pledge and donned the blue, which God helping him, he would wear to the day of his death.'[29] At one meeting he addressed over 1000 people. His contribution of £25 led the subscription for the new church building. Elizabeth became president of the ladies committee. A site for the new church was chosen on the south side of Brougham Street, around the corner from where they lived.

In August 1884 Robert chaired another meeting at Trades Hall in Carlton to form a fishmongers union. A committee of 10 was formed, with W. Mentiplay the president, Mr Slack the vice-president, Robert the treasurer and E. Jones the secretary.

> It was carried to form a Union to protect the meeting from outside hawkers, who during certain portions of the year traded on the market in a manner that was discreditable to the general body of honest dealers, and also to assist in times of illness, distress, or when the market was dull.[30]

Robert was typical in bringing a businessman's perspective to council. While his commercial activities were primarily based at the fish market, he had several enterprises in Hotham. He had opened a fish and poultry shop in Molesworth Street for a few years where his sister-in-law Louise McDonald worked. Mid-way through 1884 he took out a five-year lease on a refitted two-storey shop at 71 Queensberry Street, a few blocks east of the Town Hall, where he opened the Excelsior Auction Rooms. The ground floor contained 'the auction mart and a comfortable office, with a large store-room at the rear, while upstairs' there were several rooms 'used for placing articles of value entrusted for sale'.[31] There were plans for extensions. Robert said he intended offering the large room at the rear for the young men of Hotham, who could hold their gatherings there for free, not even paying for gas.[32]

Auctions included real estate, foodstuffs, jewellery, clothes, furniture and other household goods. Sales were advertised in the *Advertiser*, with household goods cleared each Monday. R. Langford and Co. were also money brokers, insurance agents, rent collectors and valuers, with money lent in sums from £50 to £5000. Three auctioneers were employed, who conducted sales all around the city, across the state and sometimes interstate.

The auction rooms were opened on 18 August 1884. On the same day a flag was hoisted above the Town Hall to mark Robert's election as Mayor of Hotham. He had also just finished building a new house. These were indeed very busy times.

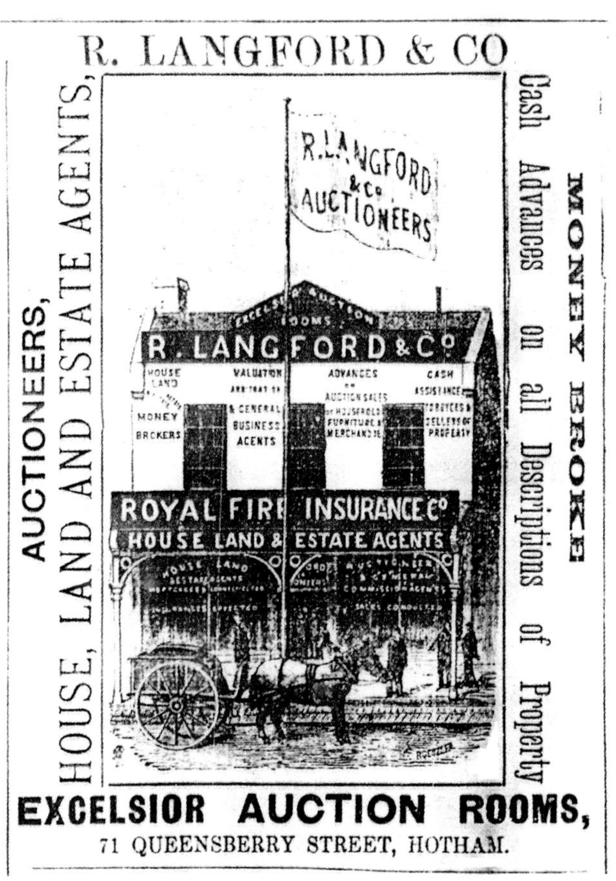

The Excelsior Auction Rooms were opened in August 1884 at 71 Queensberry Street, which was on the south side between Errol and Atkin Streets. (The building has since been demolished.) Robert employed three auctioneers, who conducted sales across the state.
SOURCE: *NORTH MELBOURNE ADVERTISER*.

6
Milton Hall

Robert and Elizabeth were prospering financially and were socially ambitious, and they decided to rebuild the house at Curran Street into something grander and more suited to entertaining. Twelve years into their marriage, they may have still hoped to start a family. Robert said at a Blue Ribbon Temperance meeting 'he was building a new house, and a large room from the money he was saving from drink', though surely he was exaggerating.[1] Turnover at the fish markets was expanding, and the move into real estate sales had apparently been successful.

In the building industry there was a basic pattern for managing the design and construction process.

> For anyone unfamiliar with building practice the procedures can be outlined thus: the client, who wants a building erected, engages an architect, who prepares plans and 'calls tenders'; the builder, one of a number who have studied the documents and worked out the costs of erection, is selected because his tender or quotation is the lowest, and it is he who signs the contract with the client. The architect watches and advises as construction proceeds, issues certificates for the builder to present to the client for payment, and sees the terms of the contract observed by both parties.[2]

A common variation to this was the omission of an architect for small houses or simple utilitarian structures, with the builder undertaking the required design work, sometimes with reference to English pattern books containing templates of standard architectural plans.

The identity of Langford's architect remains a mystery, though indirect evidence suggests it was probably either George Johnson or William Tyree.

George Raymond Johnson was born in Edmonton, near London, in 1840. He served articles under George Hall, architect to the Midlands Railway Company, then left England for Queensland, and in 1867 commenced practice in Melbourne.[3] By the early 1870s he was securing major commissions. These included the first of a long series of town halls: Hotham (1875), Albury (1882, unbuilt), Daylesford (1884),

Collingwood (1885-87), Fitzroy (1887-89, extensions), Maryborough (1888), Northcote (1890) and Kilmore (1895).[4] His massive body of work featured theatres, hospitals, large numbers of commercial buildings including the Hotham Meat Markets, and residential buildings. Two residential commissions are known to have been in North Melbourne, one being a cottage in Chetwynd Street in 1871, and another relating to the completion of two houses in Errol Street in 1875.[5]

Johnson was the architect of Hotham Town Hall, and his services were retained by council. By 1884 Robert would have been acquainted with him for several years. Similar distinctive architrave detailing to that in the upstairs drawing room/parlour of Milton Hall can be seen in extensions to the Fitzroy Town Hall, suggesting Langford's house might be the work of the same architect.[6] The Fitzroy Hall had been built in two stages, the first completed to a design by William Ellis in 1873, while the second stage was designed by Johnson and finished in 1887-90.

William Ellis was still practising in Victoria during the mid-1880s. A partial guest list survives from Robert and Elizabeth's house-warming party, and this includes a Mr Ellis, which may have been William. On balance, however, if either Johnson or Ellis was involved in the design, it is much more likely to have been Johnson, given that over a decade had passed since Ellis's work on Fitzroy Town Hall.[7]

Milton Hall in Gravesend, Kent (demolished in 1930).

SOURCE: GRAVESEND LIBRARY

Another possible architect was William Alfred Tyree, who had an office in Scotchmer Street, North Fitzroy. His father a builder, Tyree was born in London in 1850, and had arrived in Melbourne via South Australia by around 1867.[8] It is not known where he served his articles. Tyree died in November 1886 at age 36, but he left a small body of works known to have included buildings commissioned by Robert Langford. Tyree called for tenders for several cottages in Curran Street in November 1884, possibly including Kent Cottages, a pair of small houses Robert had built next to his parents' house.[9] Notices in the *Argus* in 1885 called for tenders for the erection of a terrace of six houses and a six-roomed villa for R. Langford on Flemington Road, Hotham Hill, which were not built.[10] Tyree's works were mainly domestic and in North Melbourne, an exception being a branch of the National Bank of Australasia at 270 Queens Parade, Clifton Hill, built in 1885-86. Robert and Elizabeth knew William and his wife Emily socially. Rose and Polly Tyree, almost certainly the Tyree's two daughters, attended a party Elizabeth held at her new house early in 1885. Mr and Mrs W. A. Tyree appear on council function guest lists.

Clements Langford was a builder in Melbourne at the time, and his company later became prominent in the Melbourne building industry. He was originally from Portsmouth, and had arrived in Melbourne via Launceston in 1868. There is no evidence that Clements Langford was related to the Gravesend Langfords, or that his firm was involved in the construction of Robert's new house.[11]

Construction was carried out during 1884 and completed by September. Regular passers by would have observed a standard sequence of events. After the partial demolition of the earlier building, excavators dug out the new foundations by shovel. The bluestone footings were laid, the bricklayers constructing scaffolding to build the upper floor walls. Carpenters would have constructed the internal floors and the roof structure, which was then finished by slaters. Then various other tradesmen would have visited the site to complete the interior: joiners, tilers, slaters, painters, plasterers, paperhangers, plumbers and glaziers. Paths and a garden were created along the east and north sides of the finished house, and a fernery was also built. It has been estimated that by 1888 Melbourne had 41 quarries, 120 brick and tile makers, 120 timber merchants, 480 carpenters and joiners, and 350 gas fitters and plumbers.[12] Building materials and fittings were both imported and made locally. Some of the fittings may have come from auction lots of building materials from Robert's auction rooms.

Like an aspiring Lord moving into his new manor, Robert named the new house Milton Hall, in reference to his birthplace and possibly also to the mansion of the same name built there by a town mayor, George Arnald, in 1863. Robert may have known of this through contact with family still living in Kent – several listings of the surname Langford continued to appear in the Gravesend directories through to the 1880s and beyond.

Construction proceeded in the neighbourhood in a gradual, piecemeal way. Development of the adjacent empty sites along Curran Street reflected a mixed pattern of ownership and subdivision. In 1884 a pair of double-storey terrace houses, 'Park View Terrace', was built on the north-west corner of Dryburgh and Brougham Street (now 585-87 Dryburgh Street) for a corn dealer, James Wylie. William Vaughan's 1879 house on the south side of Milton Hall along Dryburgh Street (517 Dryburgh Street) rose in value from £28 in 1884/85 to £50 in 1885/86, suggesting it may have had its existing second storey added at this time.[13]

Davis's subdivision of 1878 had created a laneway along the western property boundary. This had become known as Langfords Lane.[14]

7
The Architecture

The Rate Book citation for 1884/85 describes Milton Hall as a brick dwelling of 10 rooms, now valued at £80. The principal front elevation faced east to Dryburgh Street, presumably, like the cottage it replaced. It received praise in the local newspaper, the *Advertiser*.

> Milton Hall, which is situated in Dryburgh Street, Hotham Hill, is one of the most handsome structures in town, and for its architectural lines, is prominent to all persons passing to and fro on the Flemington Road. The building, which consists of two stories, is constructed of fine bricks with white facings, covered atop with slate roof on which is a look out, commanding an extensive view of the bay and southern suburbs. The edifice is surrounded with a verandah and a balcony, whose existence will prove a boon at all seasons of the year. The interior is splendidly furnished, the large drawing room a picture of the upholsterer's and furnisher's art. The other rooms have been finished in a superior manner, which in a measure is due to the plasterer's excellent work. In a word, Milton Hall is replete with every comfort, and has been completed in a style regardless of cost.[1]

John Laurens said it was 'an ornament and credit to the locality, and gave a decided status to the end of the street'.[2] While prominent in the immediate area, it was modest compared to some of the mansions being built by the rich on large allotments in Melbourne's eastern and outer suburbs.

No early photographs or original plans of the house appear to have survived, so the following description uses recent photos to document the architectural and decorative detail. While the building may not rank as an exceptionally rich or inventive example of domestic architecture, its decoration captures some fashions and tastes of

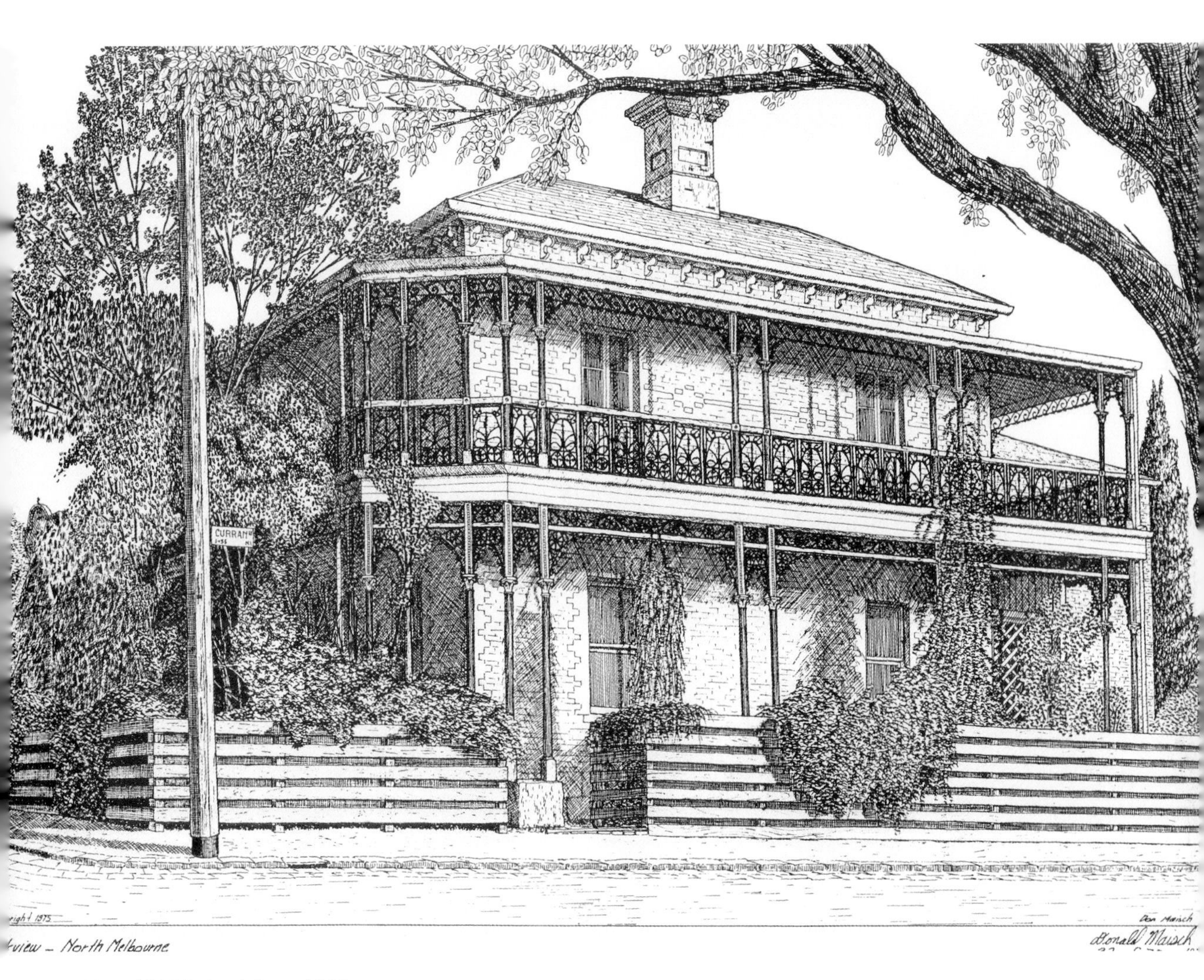

View of 519 Dryburgh Street, 1975. SOURCE: PRINT BY DONALD MAISCH.

the 1880s that typify terrace houses of the era throughout North Melbourne. It typified also common practice in aspects of its planning, construction and building materials. A description of this one house is thus also a general description of middle class North Melbourne existence, though it does also identify some idiosyncratic aspects of this particular building. The accompanying plans have been surmised from contemporary descriptions and surviving physical evidence.

The exterior

Cast Iron

The cast iron of the verandah and balcony is one of the most distinctive features of this building. Decorative cast iron used in Australia was initially imported, but local production began from the 1840s. The first iron foundry in Melbourne was that of Robert Langlands and Robert Fulton, which was established in 1842.[3] Local manufacturers of cast iron proliferated in the second half of the 19th century, with at least 42 foundries known to have existed in Melbourne.[4] Many design motifs were created in Australia, particularly as the popularity of decorative iron lace peaked during the 1880s. Unique designs were patented to prevent copying.

Langford's house incorporates seven different cast iron elements, with different patterns on the upper and lower levels. Some of these appear in a 1901 catalogue of William Stephen's Excelsior Foundry in Melbourne,[5] suggesting Stephen's foundry supplied the building's cast iron. The layout of the verandah was conceived using the baluster panel as a module. The columns are paired, the pointed spandrel arches between the pairs consist of trimmed, crudely attached pieces of the brackets seen on the east verandah, rather than separately cast individual elements. All the verandah posts are of the same length, the gentle slope of the site accommodated by mounting the posts on raised bluestone plinths along the north and west sides of the house. The wooden handrail at the upper level is a detail characteristic of Melbourne, with iron handrails typically used in Sydney and elsewhere. Also characteristic of Melbourne iron lace is the use of single verandah columns rather than the flat, open columns more common in New South Wales.

The elements would have been selected from an existing manufacturer's catalogue rather than have been specially commissioned. Some matching pieces of iron lace may be seen on nearby terrace houses along Dryburgh Street, including numbers 477-79, 407 and Parkview Terrace 485-87.

Verandah spandrels

Cast iron balustrading was also believed to have been used on the south-west lookout tower (demolished).

Balcony frieze and bracket

Balusters and baluster panels

Balcony spandrels

Verandah frieze and bracket
This design appears in the 1901 catalogue of William Stephen's Excelsior Foundry in Melbourne, (Section 4, No. 13).

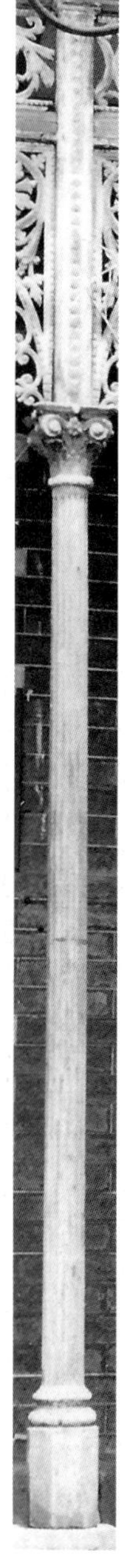

Verandah column

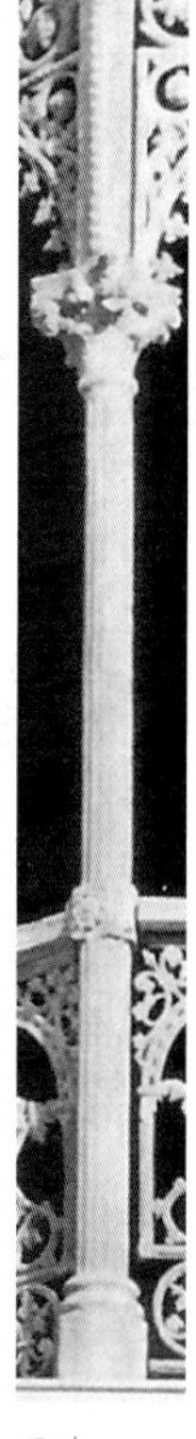

Balcony column

These verandah column designs also appear in Stephen's 1901 catalogue, (Section 14, columns no. 1 & 2).

North balcony looking east. Used in this way, iron lace provides some privacy from the street, and shading.

Masonry

External walls are of double brick construction, on bluestone footings, a construction method that resisted water penetration to the interior, avoiding the need for a protective external skin of cement rendering.

The brickwork is polychromatic, consisting of dark brown brick with cream brick quoining at the corners and around window and door openings. There were examples of this style of brickwork in Melbourne from the 1850s, but it became particularly fashionable after its use in a series of notable buildings by the architectural firm Reed and Barnes in the late 1860s, such as the Independent Church at 122-36 Collins Street, Melbourne (1867) and the mansion Rippon Lea at 192 Hotham Street, Rippon Lea (1868).[6] The bricks for the Langford house were manufactured in Melbourne. Cream bricks such as those used around the windows and doorways and in string courses are believed to have been first manufactured by John Glew in West Brunswick in the late 1850s.[7] The dark brown bricks generally known as 'Hawthorn blacks' were also made by local manufacturers at this time. The brickwork is tuck-pointed and laid in Flemish bond, except for sections of red brickwork along the west ground floor which may be from the earlier house. Champfered bricks have been used around the windows, and to form a cornice line above the ground floor verandah. There are brick flat arches above the windows and doors, with a semi-circular curved brick arch above the main stair window.

The front door facing Dryburgh Street

The ground floor windows facing Dryburgh Street feature a pair of collonettes.

Detail showing champfered brickwork around windows.

The bluestone foundation blocks are plain faced with ruled margins along the Dryburgh Street elevation, and rock faced with tuck-pointed mortar joints along the north and west facades.

The house is believed to have incorporated the west wall from Langford's original cottage, and possibly also an earlier brick kitchen to the west. Physical evidence suggests that the existing rear wing incorporating this earlier room was built in stages, though the exact sequence of development is unclear.

Surviving metal brackets suggest that the north ground floor windows had shutters.

Moulded brickwork and timber brackets form a cornice line along the verandah and balcony ceilings.

Victorian quarried stone and basalt slabs were used as steps.

Basalt base structure and footings
Inset: Detail of cast iron air vent

Roof

The chimneys feature dentiled, rendered cornices.

The original roof slates are shaped and bands were laid in a decorative fish-scale pattern. Roofing slates were usually imported during this period, the blue slate on this roof probably from Wales.[8]

External Tiling

The front verandah and the original path and Dryburgh Street were both surfaced with coloured encaustic tiles. These were imported from England, manufactured by Webb's Tileries at Rainbow Hill, Worcester, a company run by Henry Webb from 1870 until 1905.[9]

A diagonal checked pattern of soft red and cream square tiles was used on the verandah floor along the north and west sides. These were probably manufactured locally.

Tile detail

The Garden

Information about the layout of the garden and rear yard comes from an 1896 MMBW plan, which most likely shows features from the original c.1884 layout. The front garden had a symmetrical design. The main street entry was from Dryburgh Street along a short straight path paved with coloured encaustic tiles, flanked by two small oval garden beds, surrounded by narrow gravelled paths. The site would have been entirely fenced, the front fence most likely of timber pickets. Fencing was particularly necessary, as there were large numbers of stray goats roaming around Hotham Hill at the time. There would have been planting of low, flowering cottage garden plants in the front garden.

The garden on each side of the entry path from Dryburgh Street originally featured two small circular beds formed by asphalt paths. A similar, single bay front garden layout may be seen nearby at 485 and 487 Drybugh Street (487 shown below).

Early timber lattice screen with decorative timber acroteria. (South end of the east entrance verandah.)

A decorative white marble fountain dating from the 19th century survived until 1968 mid-way along the Curran Street verandah. This consisted of a bowl raised about a metre, into which water fell from a central nozzle, trickling down into a rectangular pond edged with cut bluestone beneath. The fountain was activated by a small tap located at the western side of the pond. Decorative terracotta garden edging survives on the site, which probably edged the circular garden beds at the front.

The rear yard was divided by a fence extending from the kitchen to Langford's Lane, this enclosing a paved service area with a closet located against the fence for collection of night soil. The remainder of the rear yard consisted of a paved brick area next to the main house, with a tiled path to a gate opening onto the rear lane, with a shed in the corner. There were no stables on the site, Langford using stables on the allotment behind his father's house at 13 Curran Street.

Ferneries were created as part of the initial landscaping.[10] Although not shown on the MMBW plan, these were most likely located a short distance to the west of the main house. An early ornamental lattice screen survives at the south end of the front Dryburgh Street verandah.

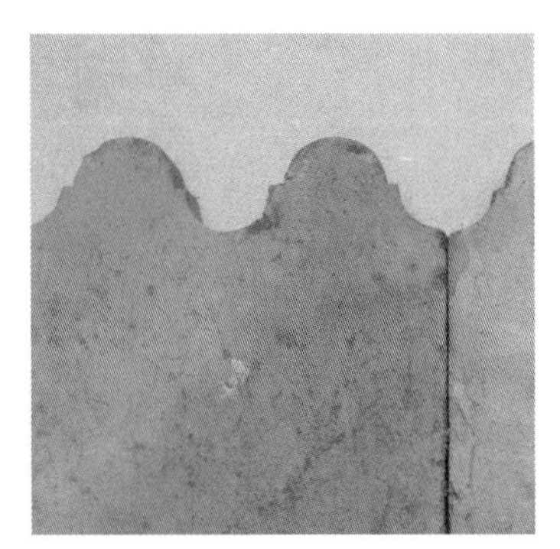

Terra cotta garden edging

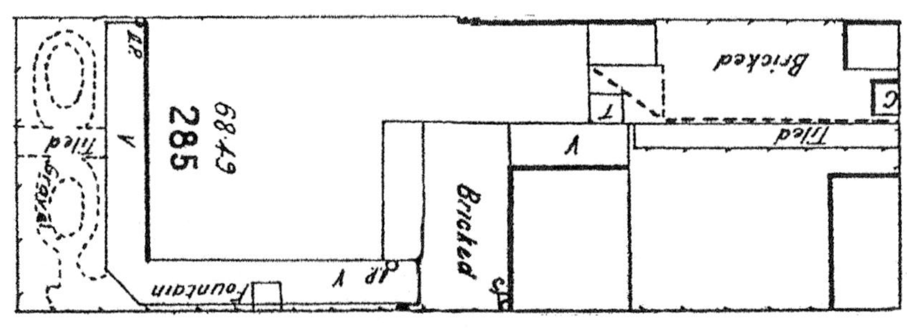

MMBW 40ft to inch plan extract, c.1896.

The Interior

The plan followed a typical pattern for a middle class house of the period. Each room contained a fireplace and received natural light. The drawing room, the climax of the formal entertainment spaces, was unusually remote from the house's formal entrance, at the top of the main stair, and approached from a formal anteroom. This had access to the balcony via four French doors. There were three or four bedrooms, one possibly intended for use as a nursery. The servants' domain was on the ground floor and consisted of the south-west corner bedroom, the kitchen west of this with a scullery and pantry in between.

Internal walls have plastered finishes, with the ceilings being lathe and plaster. A hierarchy of decoration is expressed through the building from formal to informal spaces, with the most elaborate cornice and ceiling rose plasterwork in the dining room and upper drawing room. The drawing room and first floor anteroom each feature a pair of unusual recessed alcoves with pointed arches. In the anteroom these are pointed and feature inset white marble benches. Fireplace surrounds in the principal rooms are marble, with simpler timber fittings in the rear bedrooms and study. The floors are pine on the ground floor, and Kauri pine on the first floor. The windows are standard timber-framed casement fittings, with four pairs of French doors giving access to the upper verandah. There is coloured glazing to the margins of the front door frame, main stair window and first floor south balcony door. A comprehensive investigation of the original internal decoration scheme has not been undertaken.

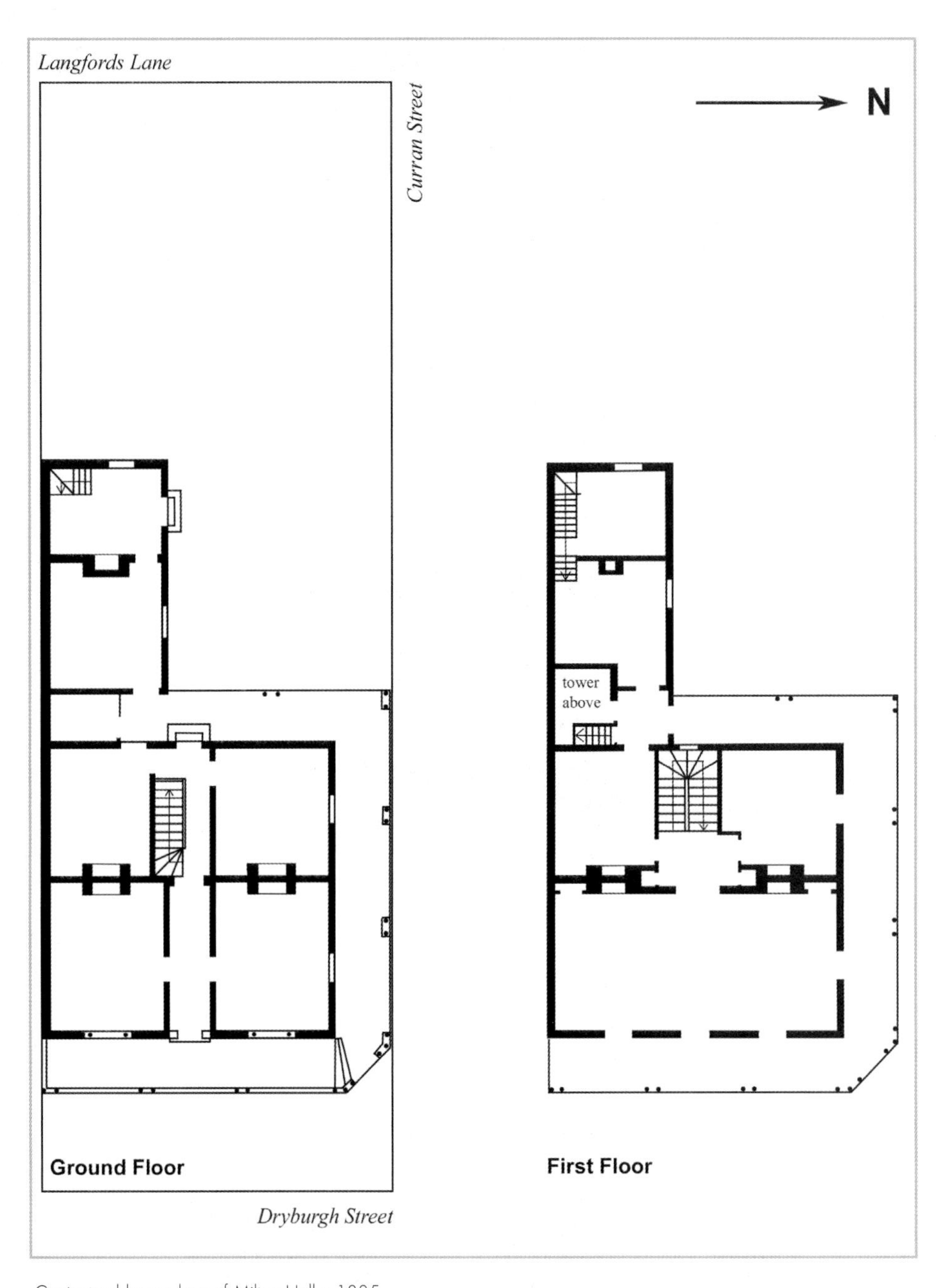

Conjectural houseplans of Milton Hall c.1885

Ground Floor Hall

Looking west through the ground floor hall.

The hallway arch features a pair of plaster consoles.

Standard internal door.

Deep moulded timber skirtings were used throughout the house.

The stair obscures the light over the rear door, which was possibly retained from the earlier cottage.

Ground Floor Bedrooms

The south-east corner bedroom.

Glazed tiles pave the ground floor fireplace hearth.

Ceiling rose

Cornice

Ceiling rose

The eastern ground floor rooms have white marble fireplaces, with deep, round profiled cornices.

South-West Ground Floor Bedroom

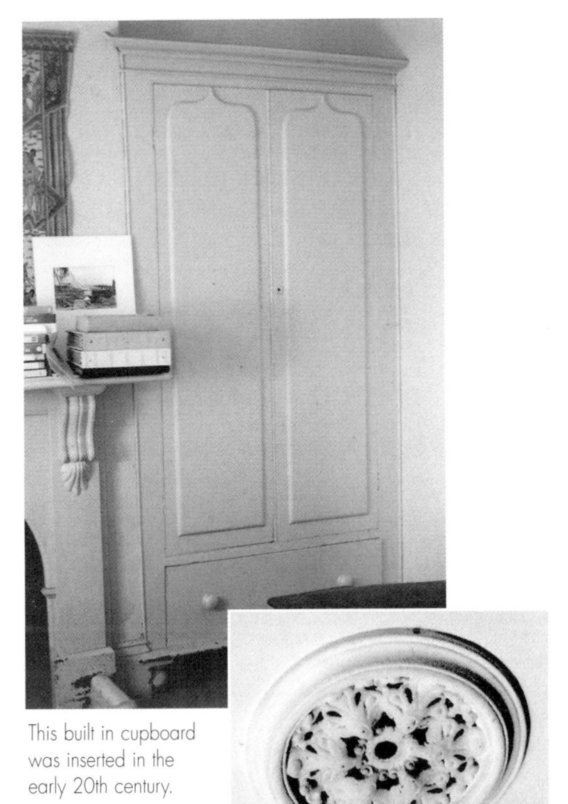

This built in cupboard was inserted in the early 20th century.

Ceiling rose

Possibly originally a servant's room, this bedroom receives only borrowed natural light.

Dining Room

Cornice

Ceiling rose

Kitchen

The room was possibly the kitchen scullery. It has a partial skillion ceiling, indicating a possible roofline before the later 1880s addition above.

Main Stair and First Floor Lobby

The north and south walls of the upstairs lobby each contains an alcove with a pointed arch and white marble bench.

View to the top of the stairs through the lobby into the drawing room.

Detail of bottom newel post.

View of the stair from the ground floor hall.

A storage cupboard beneath the main stair.

The main stairwell window

The stair window contains patterned, embossed glass, with coloured glass margins.

Drawing Room

View looking north across the drawing room.

View looking south across the drawing room.

Langford built the drawing room for entertaining. Four French doors in this room open onto the verandah. There would have originally been mirrored timber overmantels above the fireplaces. A preliminary investigation of the finishes indicates the original colour scheme consisted of blue green paint on the walls, white cornices and ceiling, and varnished brown timber graining to the skirtings and doors.

Detail of alcove console.

An alcove with an arch is at each end of the west wall.

The northern fireplace

The cornice features a grapevine motif.

The drawing room is entered through double doors featuring distinctive timber architraves.

The southern fireplace

The Kauri pine floors are a rich honey colour.

There are two ceiling roses.

Patterned tiles pave the upstairs hearths.

First Floor Bedrooms

The fireboxes are cast iron. Some have a manufacturer's inscription 'Wrights Patent Bivalve'.

An early fragment of wallpaper survives inside a built-in cupboard

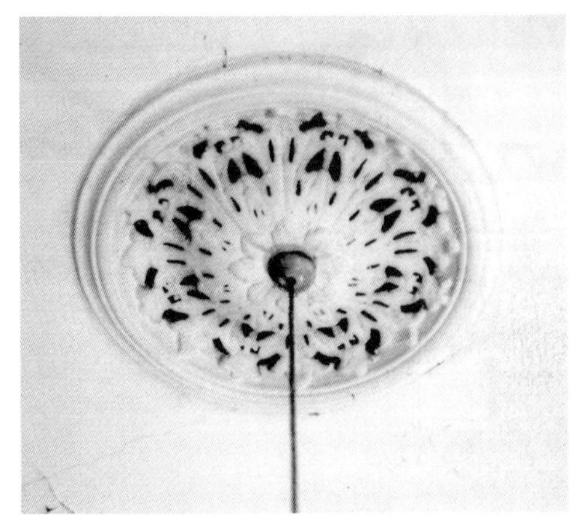

Ceiling rose in the south-west corner bedroom

Door connecting the south-west corner bedroom with the verandah. C.1920s coloured leaded glass panelling has been inserted into the doorlight.

The glazing to the door to the west balcony features marf coloured flashed glass

Door to the lookout tower stair

Tower door lock and key

The design

Typologically, this house may be read as a double terrace. A terrace house may be defined as a house in 'a row of adjoining, identical houses, or a house in such a row, each house built to its site boundaries, and usually of nineteenth century construction or design, often two storied and with iron lace decoration.' Unity of design through repetition is a defining quality, though each terrace unit need not necessarily be built at the same time. Terraces would typically contain hallways extending the full depth of the building down one side, with a stair, and rooms leading off on one side at each level. In plan Milton Hall resembles a double terrace, with rooms on both sides of the main hall.

The verandah and balcony were a response to climatic demands. The tower was visible at the rear from Curran Street, an example of a common embellishment to boom style residences, often built for the practical purpose of concealing water tanks, though this tower appears to have been whimsical. From the tower and the balcony, the roar of the lions could be heard across Royal Park at Melbourne Zoo.

Not quite right

A number of features about the design and construction of the building suggest the architect was working within some very particular design constraints, and/or was perhaps new to designing domestic buildings. These are:

- The asymmetrical alignment of the verandah structure in relation to the facade along Dryburgh Street
- The relatively narrow dimensions of the entry lobby and main stair. A broader, more open hallway and stairwell might have been expected in such an imposing house, although the narrow site places some constraints on internal planning.
- The main stair has been built obscuring the doorlight of the rear door. An explanation for this could be that the 1884 building incorporated the west wall of Langford's original cottage, the door and doorlight being existing elements incorporated into the new building.
- The main stair window is circular arched in form, yet has been fitted with a square topped window frame on the interior side.
- Use of lathe and plaster in upstairs internal walls instead of brick, a weaker structural arrangement than brick walls.
- Although similar in colour and design, the two fireplaces in the upstairs drawing room do not exactly match. A possible conjecture for this is that these and other fittings came from auction lots of building materials from Robert Langford's auction rooms, and this pair may have happened to become available at the time of construction.

8
Mayor of Hotham

Mayors were chosen by council after each annual election and served for one year. Most of the other councillors had already occupied the position, and of the three who had not, Robert was the longest serving. (In the 1883 elections William Cook and James Steel had replaced James Carroll and Hugh Lennon.) Cook nominated Robert Langford for election at the meeting held on 18 August. Robert's interest had been canvassed three months earlier, so the nomination was no surprise to Elizabeth. There were rumours of his candidature in the local press.

Accepting the role, Robert said that 'When he arrived eight years ago in the town and passed the hall he had little thought that he would ever become a Councillor let alone the Mayor, but now that he had obtained the honour he would do his best to carry out the details in connection with high position.'[1]

The role was largely honorary. According to the *Advertiser,* the Mayor 'should have a firm character, shrewd business attainments, and on all occasions be able to express himself with some aptitude, and credit in keeping with the high position he occupies'.[2] It meant chairing council meetings, certifying the council minute book and presiding at a busy calendar of social events. It required mediation and negotiation skills, and 'not being too thin-skinned'. The Mayor received an allowance of £100 and use of rooms at the Town Hall. It was expected that the Mayor's wife would act as hostess at council functions. Robert was 36. Elizabeth was 30.

The first large function the Mayor and Mayoress hosted was not a council event, but a house-warming party for Milton Hall. The venue for the party had to be changed to the Town Hall after they invited 180 guests. It was probably the largest event Elizabeth had ever hosted and it set the scale and tone for their subsequent entertaining. The evening began at 9 pm with a program of dancing in the main hall. This stately room had a lofty double height ceiling and was elegantly decorated with 'a French composite order' of plaster pilasters along the walls.[3] Guests included various 'well-known local residents'. The women arrived in costumes of coloured satin, muslin, velvet and broche, trimmed with lace, ribbon, pearls and flowers; large bustles were the fashion at this time. The men wore sombre black dress suits, with white shirts, vests, cravats and gloves. Bartlings' five-piece band played music on the fern-lined stage as the dancers moved across the polished timber floors. Men smoked, played cards and discussed politics in the Mayor's room.[4]

Supper was served at midnight, on six large tables in an adjacent lecture room. Menu cards outlined a substantial meal including *turkey au truffles* and larded guinea fowls. Waiters darted amongst the seated guests serving wine and champagne. 'Ample time having been allowed to bring each defunct member of the poultry yard under review', Robert as chairman introduced the toasts. They drank to 'The Queen', then 'Our Guests'. Mr Angus Maclean toasted 'prosperity to the town of Hotham'. Attention shifted to Robert and Elizabeth as Dr Rose MLA praised the 'Host and Hostess'. He wished them 'long life and prosperity', and hoped they might even repeat the ceremony when the previous Mayor Thomas Pilkington was presented with a silver cradle on the birth of a son while in office, according to an old English custom. Robert responded while Elizabeth looked 'very becoming' in a 'toilette of pale blue nun's veiling, full bodice and loops of narrow pale blue ribbon'. Not forgetting the purpose of the gathering, fellow councillor Mr John Laurens MLA proposed a toast to the architect and builders of Milton Hall. Afterwards the music and dancing continued until 4.30 am.[5]

Elizabeth was encouraged by the success of their first big function. She was young and fashionable, and could afford to lavishly provide for her guests, helped no doubt by Robert's market connections. She began holding regular receptions in the Mayor's rooms at 3 pm on the last Monday of each month. The first was in late September and attracted 80 women. It was regarded as an innovation.

> [It was], so far as we remember, the first time in the history of the colony that the Mayoress of any suburb has similarly received the ladies of any municipality ... The sideboard was laden with tempting entremets, and the occasion very much resembled a drawing room reunion. It is the intention of the Mayoress to hold a reception the last Monday in each month, and no doubt the slight stiffness attendant on the initial effort will entirely disappear, as the ladies become better known to each other.[6]

A profile and portrait of Mr Robert Langford, Mayor of Hotham, was published in the *Melbourne Bulletin* on 2 October 1885.
SOURCE: STATE LIBRARY OF VICTORIA.

The magnificent Hotham Town Hall was the venue for some of Robert and Elizabeth's grandest parties, including the housewarming for Milton Hall (attended by 180), and the Mayor's Ball (attended by over 300).
SOURCE: STATE LIBRARY OF VICTORIA.

Robert supported her at the next reception, but the 'slight stiffness' had dissipated and the receptions became increasingly popular. Friends and visitors mingled and networked as maids carried in plates of delicacies. The January reception had to be cancelled after Elizabeth became 'seriously indisposed' for a week. In February the guests braved whirling dust storms to attend. By April over 130 leading ladies from Hotham and across Melbourne were leaving their calling cards. Her last reception on 26 July was the most successful of them all, with over 250 visitors leaving their cards.[7] It was commented that Elizabeth was able to 'infuse among her visitors a feeling of good spirit and ease'.[8] Her experiment had been successful, and was noted in the society journal *Table Talk*.[9] Mayoresses in Prahran and other suburbs began holding similar receptions.

Mention of hope that Robert might be presented with a casket to mark the birth of a child during his term as Mayor at the housewarming party is the only direct hint that the couple may have been hoping to have children at the time. Elizabeth's death certificate lists two stillborn babies, John and Cissie. It is possible that Elizabeth had fallen pregnant during the year when Robert was Mayor. There are references to her being 'seriously indisposed' in January and again in June.

A regular guest at many of their functions was their friend from Faversham,

James Pierce. He was still running a tobacco shop in Elizabeth Street, and successfully gained a seat in the Bourke Ward of Melbourne City Council in November 1884. A few years later he became a member of the Legislative Assembly.[10]

With the house renovations complete, they were ready to entertain at home. Early in the new year they put on a fish and oyster dinner for 75 guests, predominantly council associates. Robert was 'sorry his house was not six times larger, so that he might invite six times as many guests'.

> After the various courses of fish and oysters had been removed, light confectionery, fruit, champagne and wines were dispensed ... As each of the gentlemen were accompanied by their ladies, the room was cleared and dancing was indulged in till an early hour. Songs and recitations were given in the splendidly furnished drawing room.[11]

The drawing room was on the first floor overlooking Dryburgh Street. On warm summer nights the guests could wander onto the balconies, taking the breeze and views across to Royal Park. The dining room was small, but there was space in the rear yard for a marquee. Although it was said he was a teetotaller, Robert maintained a wine cellar. It would have been somewhat embarrassing when the theft of some spirits by a Mr McInnis was reported in the *Advertiser*.[12]

Political intrigue was not restricted to the Town Hall. What was to become a long-running dispute was underway at the Fish Markets. Joseph Hill ran a fish shop at 12 Swanston Street, and in June 1881 was granted permission to sell by auction in the Fish Markets.[13] Late in 1884 he wrote to the MCC Markets Committee requesting that he be granted a sales stand inside the Fish Market. He did this with the support of a group of regional fishermen from Queenscliffe and Geelong, who sent a deputation to the Mayor of Melbourne to discuss the matter. The fishermen felt other salesmen at the fish markets were frequently selling their catches privately for sub-optimal prices, rather than by auction. They felt Hill would better serve their interests. The Markets Committee was sympathetic to Hill, initially reporting to the inspector that a stand should be made available to Hill if room could be found for it. The other salesmen, including Langford, all opposed this, moving to block Hill's entry. A letter of protest was received from Messrs Denton, Paice, Langford, Mentiplay, Renouf and Richie complaining there was not enough room in the market for an additional stall. This was confirmed by the inspector, which resulted in the Committee refusing Hill's application.[14]

Hill took over a vacated exterior shop or stall, where he began making wholesale sales even though he was only allowed to sell retail at that location. In a letter endorsed by Langford, John Paice wrote to the Committee in complaint.[15] The Committee remained sympathetic to Hill, particularly in light of the fact that Hill's fish sales at the South Melbourne Market were almost as large in volume as those of all the Fish Market salesmen combined, but was unable to offer him a stand despite receiving regular applications from him over the next few years. The dispute dragged on until Hill was finally granted a stall in August 1889.[16] It received some coverage in the press, including a reference in the *North Melbourne Advertiser*.[17]

Robert's younger brother Richard moved to New South Wales where he married a Ms Mary Livingstone. His remaining siblings, however, lived close by, and with a growing list of nephews and nieces, Robert and Elizabeth enjoyed playing Uncle Bob and Aunty Lizzie. On 16 January 1885 Elizabeth hosted a children's fancy dress ball at Milton Hall for nephew Arthur John, who had recently turned five. Fancy dress was a popular form of festivity for children and adults, and fancy dress balls were periodically held in the Town Hall. Robert and Elizabeth had attended the Hotham Private Quadrille Society's annual plain and fancy dress ball the previous September. The Mayor of Melbourne had hosted a children's fancy dress ball the previous November, which might have given Elizabeth the idea.

More then 70 fairies, flower girls, red riding hoods, pirates, cricketers, sailors, and jockeys began arriving at eight o'clock.

> The space between the ferneries and the residence was covered with an awning from which depended many coloured lanterns whose variegated lights cast a shadow of mystery over the whole scene ... Dancing was the chief attraction, and to the strains of Zeplin's band the juveniles performed polkas, waltzes and lancers in a manner that would be envied by many a senior 'who fancies he can dance.' Refreshments were served throughout the evening, and the wants of the visitors were well attended to by the Mayoress, who was ubiquitous in her endeavours to make the young people at home. Singing and music were interspersed between the dancing, which was held in a miniature ballroom at the rear of the hall, which was thrown open to the guests, who roamed *ad lititum* through the well appointed rooms.[18]

There may have been cake on the carpet, fingerprints on the walls, and the occasional tearful moment, but overall the party was another of Elizabeth's great successes. A photographer took portraits of all those present. The children departed at midnight while the adults partied on upstairs.

Robert was a patron of the Hotham Football Club, now the North Melbourne Football Club. It played the emerging local game of Australian Rules football, which had become popular across Victoria and some of the other colonies. The Hotham Club had been formed in 1869 and amalgamated with the Hotham Cricket Club in 1882.[19] Its colours were blue and white. Robert would have watched the players at local matches.

In March, the club's Annual General Meeting clashed with a regular council night.

> The Mayor said he should feel obliged if the council would permit the ordinary business to take priority of the receiving of letters &c., as he had to be present as chairman at a meeting of the Hotham Football Club, and therefore wished to get away as soon as possible.[20]

Five hundred members and supporters were present at the meeting, including Councillors Fogarty, Steel and Pilkington. Robert and Dr Beaney MLC, Dr Rose MLA, and John Laurens MLA were elected patrons. (Robert was also a patron of the Royal Park Football Club.) The ongoing need to improve the drainage at the club's recreational reserve was discussed. Councillor Pilkington noted the council had already obtained a grant of land for the Club, and assured the meeting that the club could rely on council's full support in lobbying the Public Works Department for further improvements to the site. Football had a wide community following, so the recreational reserve was an electorally pertinent cause.[21]

The Hotham team toured South Australia in May 1885. They played against Sandhurst in July, winning 15 goals to nil. Afterwards the Hotham side put on a dinner for the visitors, chaired by Robert in the Town Hall. Sixty were in attendance.[22] On 25 May he hosted another dinner for 150 in honour of the Hotham and

Elizabeth's juvenile fancy dress ball in January 1885 may have been inspired by a children's fancy dress ball held by the Mayor of Melbourne several months earlier. Over 70 children arrived at Milton Hall for an evening of singing, dancing and music.
SOURCE: STATE LIBRARY OF VICTORIA.

HOTHAM FOOTBALL TEAM — 1884

Taken in Adelaide

Back Row—A. TODD, R. HOUSTON, J. GARDINER, GRAY, O'BRIEN, CLEMENTS, POLLOCK (Adelaide)
Third Row—CHERRY, PERKINS, McCRACKEN, BUNCLE, H. TODD, TANKARD, LANG, NEILY, MORRIS.
Second Row—WILL JOHNSTON, RILEY, BAILEY, SYKES, PETERS, FLOWERS, NAINN.
Front Row—WAL JOHSTON, EMMS, RAE, ALESSIO

Robert was a patron of the Hotham Football Club, now the North Melbourne Football Club. This portrait of the team was taken while they were on tour in Adelaide in 1884. Robert hosted a number of dinners in the Town Hall for the team and visiting sides.
SOURCE: NORTH MELBOURNE LIBRARY

visiting Port Adelaide and Geelong teams. It was another occasion when he wished the Town Hall was larger so that more could join the festivities.

Councillors were often also Justices of the Peace. Robert had begun appearing behind the bench as a 'JP' before he became Mayor. He particularly disapproved of the coarse men and youths who tended to loiter around the front of the town hall making nuisances of themselves and he showed 'a decided determination to put down all manner of unruly conduct'. He had some direct experience of such behaviour when he was attacked in the street in April 1885. After renting in nearby Molesworth Street, James and Euphemia had moved to Curran Street with their five children by the early months of 1885. In court 'Mr R. Langford stated that he was talking at his brother's building at Curran Street when the prisoners came up and made use of foul language. He requested them to go away, but they refused to do so, and after using more bad language they rushed at him and pulled his collar off'.[23] The defendants were fined 2s 6d each plus 2s 6d costs.

Throughout the mayoral year, Robert and Elizabeth's social calendar was crammed with functions and meetings. There were invitations to council events around Melbourne as well as calls for support from numerous neighbourhood causes. Robert was a committee member of the Art Union, patron of the Thespian Amateur

Dramatic Club and a member of the Hotham Board of Advice overseeing local schools. The Board of Advice, of which James Langford was also a member, met every month, and also organised events such as children's excursions. Its annual prize giving function in the Town Hall typically attracted over 1000, and Robert donated a £10 prize for neat workbooks for the 1885 awards.[24] Robert chaired a meeting to form a local volunteer defence corps at which 70 people enrolled, and he organised a lecture at the Town Hall in aid of the poor.[25]

It was customary for the Mayor to mark the end of his term with a function and the ball Robert and Elizabeth put on in the Town Hall became legendary. Four hundred invitations were issued for the evening of Friday 3 July, the guest list encompassing every prominent local citizen as well as leading figures from councils around Melbourne. Hotham buzzed with anticipation.

> From eight to shortly after nine o'clock carriages and cabs drove to the steps and deposited the guests, who soon were lost sight of by the eager crowd of some 200 persons who gathered around the main entrance to catch a glimpse of the fair forms enveloped in fur coverings.[26]

The footpath and main entry steps were carpeted, while overhead coloured lights lit a fabric canopy. Over 300 guests arrived in their dress suits and finest evening wear, the watching crowd not dispersing until midnight. There were various newspaper reporters present.

The guests made their way to the ballroom in the main hall. 'A maid in waiting announced the guests to the Mayor and Mayoress, who, upstanding, received each with a cordial "How are you?" and a shake of the hand.' Mrs Langford wore a 'moss green plush skirt, with bodice and flowing train of rose pink broche satin, relieved with tuffets of moss green and pink feathers, trimmed with green and pink lace.' The hall was decorated with national flags arranged in groups, and there were eight massive mirrors on the north and east walls flanked by curtains and tapestries. From nine o'clock onwards, lines of figures danced in the packed hall to the music of the seven-piece band hidden behind fernery on the stage. The council chamber had been converted into a drawing room, complete with lounges and a pianist. Other rooms were used for card games and smoking while 'the various nooks and recesses throughout the building were quite as much sought after'. Supper had to be held in a series of separate rooms because there were so many people present. [27]

Praise for the evening was unequivocal. 'Mr and Mrs Langford can lay claim to having given the best appointed and most enjoyable ball ever held in the history of the Town of Hotham.'

Anyone who had doubted Robert's commitment to council during the first two years of his term would have to agree his performance as Mayor was outstanding. By all accounts he had been a hard working, efficient and supremely hospitable Mayor, 'the right man for the right place'. He and Elizabeth proved to be effective social organisers as well as good company. Robert far out-spent his £100 allowance, subsidising all additional expenditure on entertainment himself. 'We venture to assert that six times the annual allowance would not cover the outlay.'[28] He missed only two meetings over the whole year, one on account of Mrs Langford being 'indisposed' during June. His pervasive community involvements owed much to his ability as an effective chairman. He lobbied for the enlargement of the Town Hall, though this was not approved until 1886.[29]

Works to fill in the North Melbourne Swamp and some of the eastern side of the Moonee Ponds Creek had opened up a large section of adjacent land to development. A series of new streets was created in 1884 on the eastern side of the creek, named after sitting councillors, including Henderson, Reynolds, Green, Steel, with the longest named after the Mayor, Langford Street. Robert also purchased some land in the area, Allotment 1 along Macauley Road.

Hotham had come a long way since the Langfords had first moved to the area in the early 1870s. Describing its development, the journalist Edmund Finn wrote:

> Looking around you, compare it as it is now with what it was not many years ago, when all the country around by the Royal Park and the other Hill of Hotham, revealed a vista of hill and dale, well wooded and grassed, well suited for a delightful rambling excursion. The perspective now is an untold treasure, planted in the soil, and cropping up in splendid mansions, handsome villas, busy marts, spacious streets, squares, parks and gardens, and stately churches – all these practical evidences of civilisation 'where flourished once a forest fair.'[30]

The Mayor's Ball had been such a success that a committee was immediately formed to organise a Return Ball for a month later. This attracted 130 couples. Elizabeth was presented with an album of photographs of the children at her fancy dress ball and a bracelet 'of 30 diamonds, 24 in the circle in the centre and three down each side of the cluster, set in a thick band of gold'. Robert said 'his wife who had received such chaste gifts had always been his right hand supporter and help-meet and in fact he would have been at a loss to bring the various entertainments to a successful result without her.' There were three cheers for the Mayoress, then the Mayor.[31]

Robert's last function as Mayor was an oyster supper in the upstairs rooms of the Town Hall on 8 August, when 120 gentlemen drank light wine and worked their way through 200 dozen Stewart Island oysters. After the health of the Mayor was toasted, Robert vowed 'if elected Mayor in the future of Hotham he would carry out his entertainments on a greater scale of liberality as he had by experience learned how to work with better results'.[32]

His three-year term as councillor ended in July of 1885 and he was re-elected without opposition. James Steel succeeded him as Mayor at the first meeting of the new council on 10 August. Robert presented the town officials each with a monogrammed pipe as a momentum of his year in office. On behalf of Mrs Langford, Town Clerk Charles Randall was presented with a silver mounted Russian pocket book and cigar case, in appreciation of his assistance in helping her organise social functions in the Town Hall.[33]

Robert and Elizabeth maintained close contact with Elizabeth's relatives in Maryborough and visitors from Maryborough and Carisbrook regularly appeared on their guest lists. Some of her own nephews had attended the children's fancy dress ball. William Miller was elected Mayor of Carisbrook[34] the same day Robert's term as Mayor finished. There was still something of the showman in him. He would bring to the annual Maryborough New Year's Highland Sports a big swinging boat for people to ride in.

Robert's term as Mayor changed his outlook and through council, he and Elizabeth developed a wide social circle drawn from the spheres of business and government. They were in the social columns of the local newspaper and *Table Talk*. A profile of Robert including an engraved portrait appeared on the front page of the *Melbourne Bulletin* on 2 October 1885. He became socially notable, a man about town, though he does not appear to have been associated with gentlemen's clubs such as the Melbourne Club, the various Masonic lodges or to have been a guest at Government House. He gained an understanding of the mechanics of both local and colonial government. In becoming Mayor Robert had risen as high as he could in the context of Hotham Council and had taken on a very taxing round of social obligations. Robert and Elizabeth were developing wider interests.

9
The Curran Street estates

The Langford family began settling close together in Curran Street from the late 1870s, and their properties formed a distinct cluster of associated estates.

The Curran Street presence had begun in 1879, when Robert Langford bought the block on the corner with Dryburgh Street, where he built a small cottage. The following year he also purchased 13 Curran Street (Milton Cottage) for his parents John and Harriet, building stables at the rear of the allotment. In 1884 Robert decided to rebuild his cottage into Milton Hall. At about that time, James and Euphemia had started constructing a house at the other end of the street, at number 21 (now 27), which they called 'Gravesend'. In 1885/86 Robert subdivided the northern part of 13 Curran Street, building two attached cottages named 'Kent Cottages' next to his parent's home. This sequence of properties named after the family's home town – Milton Hall, Milton Cottage, Gravesend, Kent Cottages[1] – was further expanded in 1888/89 with the construction of two small cottages at 1 and 2 Curran Place, behind 9-13 Curran Street. Two of Euphemia Langford's siblings, James and Mary Rea, later also moved to Curran Street with their families, with Robert's sister Harriet moving to 2 Curran Place in 1889.[2]

In about 1884 Robert also bought some land around the corner along Flemington Road (between Dryburgh and Melrose Streets).[3] He was apparently thinking of building some speculative terrace housing. On 30 January 1885, and again on 2 May 1885, the architect William Tyree invited tenders for the erection of 'six terrace houses and a six-roomed villa at Flemington Road, Hotham Hill' for R. Langford.[4] The proposed development did not proceed, however, and by 1888 the land had been sold. The timber corner shop on the corner of Dryburgh Street and Flemington Road was probably built on one of Langford's blocks. (It first appears in rate books in 1887/88 as a four-roomed timber dwelling in 1888 belonging to a cordial maker, William John

Hare, and was described as a shop and dwelling run by Mrs W. J. Hare the following year.[5])

The traditional pattern of extended family members living close together derives from mutual needs for social and financial support. In other contexts this may be reflected in particular building types, such as large courtyard houses, family compounds, or single residences designed to accommodate multiple households. In this case accommodation was acquired as needed by purchasing a series of nearby sites and subdividing an existing property.

Address	*Name*	*Built*	*Initial occupant*	*Owner*
519 Dryburgh Street	Milton Hall	1880	Robert Langford	Robert Langford 1880–86
1 Curran Place		1888/89	Arthur Curtis	Robert Langford
2 Curran Place		1888/89	Harriet Johnson	Robert Langford
3 Curran Place	(stables)	c.1880?	Used by Robert & James Langford	Robert Langford
9 Curran Street	Kent Cottages	1885/86	Charles Wright	Robert Langford
11 Curran Street	Kent Cottages	1885/86	James Munro	Robert Langford
13 Curran Street	Milton Cottage/ Milton Villa	1871	James Coffey, then John & Harriet Langford	Robert Langford
16 Curran Street	Vacant land		–	James Langford
27 Curran Street	Gravesend	1884/85	James Langford	James Langford
Land, Flemington Road	Vacant Land	Owned 1884–86	–	Robert Langford

Subdivision of Allotment 7

9-13 Curran Street and 1-3 Curran Place developed with the gradual subdivision by Robert Langford of a larger crown allotment, Allotment 7 (Section 88 of the Parish of Jika Jika). The evolution of the existing structures on this site is shown on the plans below. It began with the construction of 13 Curran Street by James Coffey in c.1871. (The stables were built some time before 1890, and are probably contemporary with Milton Hall.)

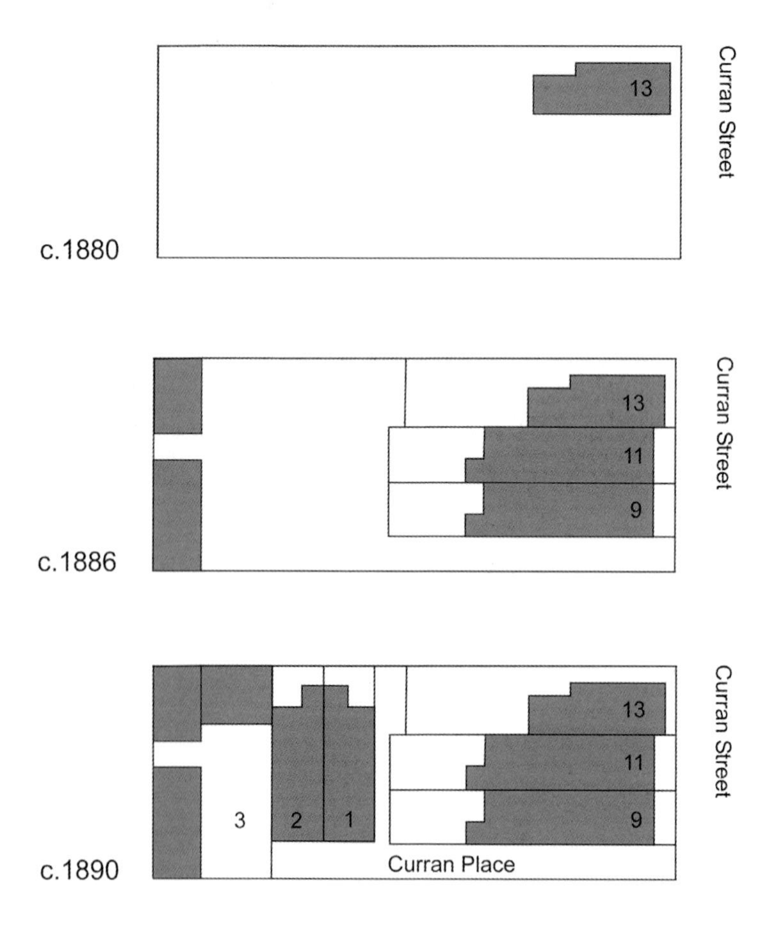

9-11 Curran Street, North Melbourne

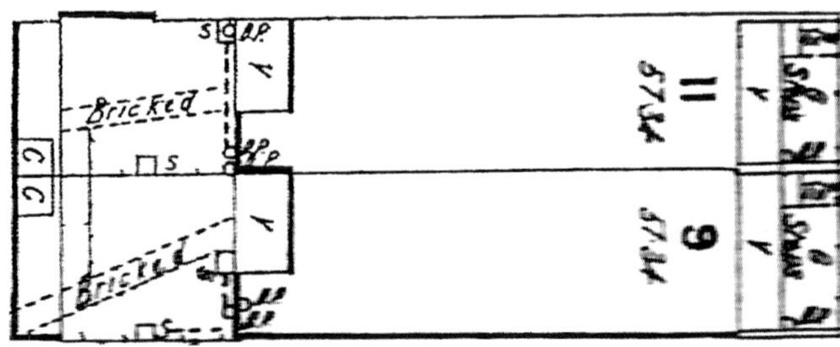

MMBW Plan c.1896

These attached single-storey cottages were constructed by Robert Langford in c.1885/86.[6] The following tender notice appeared in the *Argus* in November 1884 and most likely related to these two cottages. 'Tenders wanted for 2 cottages, Curran Street, HOTHAM PLANS W. Tyree, Scotchmer Street, North Fitzroy'.[7] The name 'Kent Cottages' in the parapet refers to Langford's birthplace in Kent. Number 9 was occupied by Charles Curtis from 1893–94 onwards. From the late 1890s number 11 was occupied by James Rea, a brother-in law of James Langford. Robert Langford retained ownership until 1900, when he sold them to confectioner, Alfred W. Allen.

13 Curran Street, North Melbourne

Milton Cottage, in Gravesend, Kent.

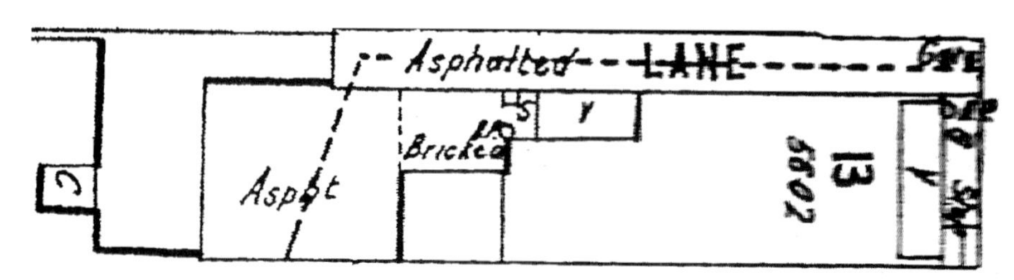

MMBW Plan c.1896

This one-storey rendered brick cottage was constructed in c.1871. It was acquired by Robert Langford c.1881 from James Coffey, who had originally purchased the site at the Crown auction in 1867. It was then occupied by Langford's parents, Harriet and John Langford. After their deaths, he sold the property in 1900 to confectioner Alfred W. Allen, along with 9 and 11 Curran Street and 1–3 Curran Place.[8] Contemporary documents refer to the building as Milton Cottage and Milton Villa. There was also a house with that name in Milton, Kent.[9]

1 & 2 Curran Place, North Melbourne

This pair of attached one-storey brick cottages was built by Robert Langford on small sites created by the further subdivision of the original block of 13 Curran Street. The subdivision included the creation of Curran Place along the eastern site of the original allotment boundary to provide access to these new properties from Curran Street and the division of the stable area to the south at 3 Curran Place. From 1890 until the late 1920s, number 2 was occupied by Robert Langford's sister, Harriet Johnson. From about 1900 to 1904, the occupants of number 1 were the sister-in-law of James Langford, Mary Emma Rogan [Rea] and cab driver husband Francis, and their children. Robert Langford sold the properties along with 9, 11 and 13 Curran Street in 1900 to confectioner Alfred W. Allen.

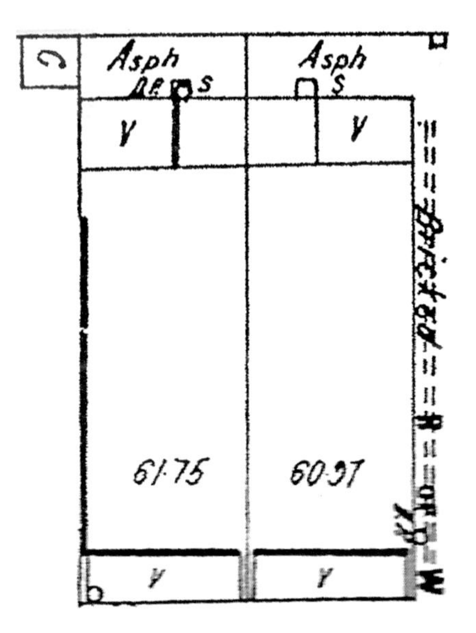

MMBW Plan c.1896

3 Curran Place, North Melbourne

Howrie's forge at 2 (A) Curran Street.
SOURCE: NORTH MELBOURNE LIBRARY

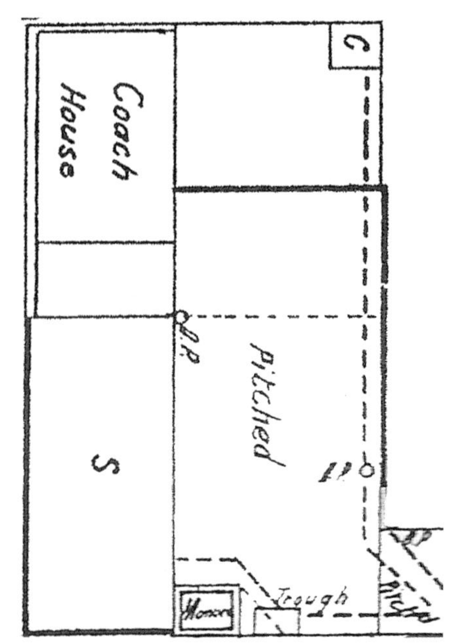

MMBW Plan c.1896

This land was first acquired by Robert Langford c.1880 as part of a larger site formerly including 9, 11, 13 Curran Street, 1 and 2 Curran Place and the laneway itself, which corresponded to the boundaries of the original Crown Allotment. The existing property boundaries date from a second stage of subdivision by Langford, which occurred c. 1888. Stables were recorded at this address from 1888, though these had probably been constructed prior to the subdivision. By 1895 the site contained brick stables and a coach house (now demolished), on the southern side of a pitched yard. Used as stables by Robert Langford (and family), Robert retained these stables after later moving to Hawthorn and then Romsey. Land also owned by his brother James at 16 Curran Street from 1894 was possibly used for horses.

In 1889 the buildings were almost burnt down when stables on an adjacent property caught fire.

> Mr R. Langford has forwarded a cheque for two guineas towards the funds of the North Melbourne and Hotham Fire Brigades respectively for their successful exertions in saving his stable, horses, &c., at the fire at Hotham Hill on Tuesday evening ... A fire broke out in a stable adjoining those of Mr Langford's buildings in Curran Street, Hotham Hill, early on Wednesday morning. The North Melbourne and Hotham Hill brigades attended and after some difficulty subdued the flames as Flemington Road was the nearest point from whence water could be obtained. Two horses were burnt to death and the building was completely consumed. The stable was occupied by a Mr. Skinner, and owned by Mr. Thomas Brown, hotelkeeper, who it is stated is uninsured.[10]

From 1889 there was a farrier nearby in Curran Street. In that year, blacksmith James Howrie built a small brick forge on the triangular site at the eastern end of Curran Street. He advertised 'J. Howrie, Farrier' in the pediment above the corner doorway, which faced east along Flemington Road toward the approaching traffic. Howrie occupied the forge until deciding to lease it out in around 1900.

Robert Langford retained ownership of these properties and 9-13, and 1-2 Curran Place until 1900, when he sold them to confectioner Alfred W. Allen. By the 1950s, brick stable buildings remained on the site, which was being used as a garage and store.[11] The property was redeveloped for residential use in the early 1980s.

27 Curran Street, North Melbourne

This two-storey, rendered brick house was built in c.1885 by James Langford.[12] A tender notice appearing in the *Argus* in June 1885 possibly relates to this house. 'J. Rankine, architect, Imperial Chambers, Bank Place, invites TENDERS two-storey brick RESIDENCE, Curran Street, Hotham.'[13] The street facade is thought to have originally been polychromatic brick, with a cast iron verandah and balcony, visually relating to Milton Hall at the eastern end of the street and built at around the same time. Extensions were added to the rear over the following decade. The finished building was occupied by James Langford and his family of nine children from 1885 until after James's death in 1911, when it was sold the following year to Richard Fry. A small brick cottage had been constructed at the rear by 1895, and this may have been occupied by groomsmen looking after the stables at 3 Curran Place. When the properties along Curran Street received street numbering in 1888/89, the house that was originally number 21 changed to 27 in 1894/95. The rear cottage was demolished in c. 2001. James also owned a vacant allotment across the street at 16 Curran Street, where the family may have grazed their horses. The house was purchased by adjacent St Aloysius College in 1999.

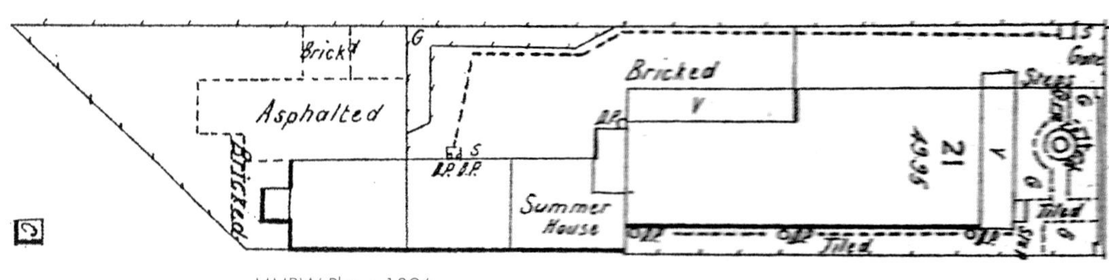

MMBW Plan c.1896

1890s Field Survey Notebooks

As part of the project to construct a reticulated sewerage system for Melbourne in the 1890s, surveyors from the Melbourne Metropolitan Board of Works (MMBW) plotted the location of the buildings in each of Melbourne's suburbs on a series of maps in preparation for the installation of piped connections. The surveyors measured the dimensions of the structures on every block, which they recorded in field survey notebooks. Shown below are the field notebook entries for the Langfords' properties along Curran Street. These are not drawn to scale, but show detailed annotations including the number of storeys, dimensions and the function of outbuildings. They provide a detailed snapshot of the layout of each site.

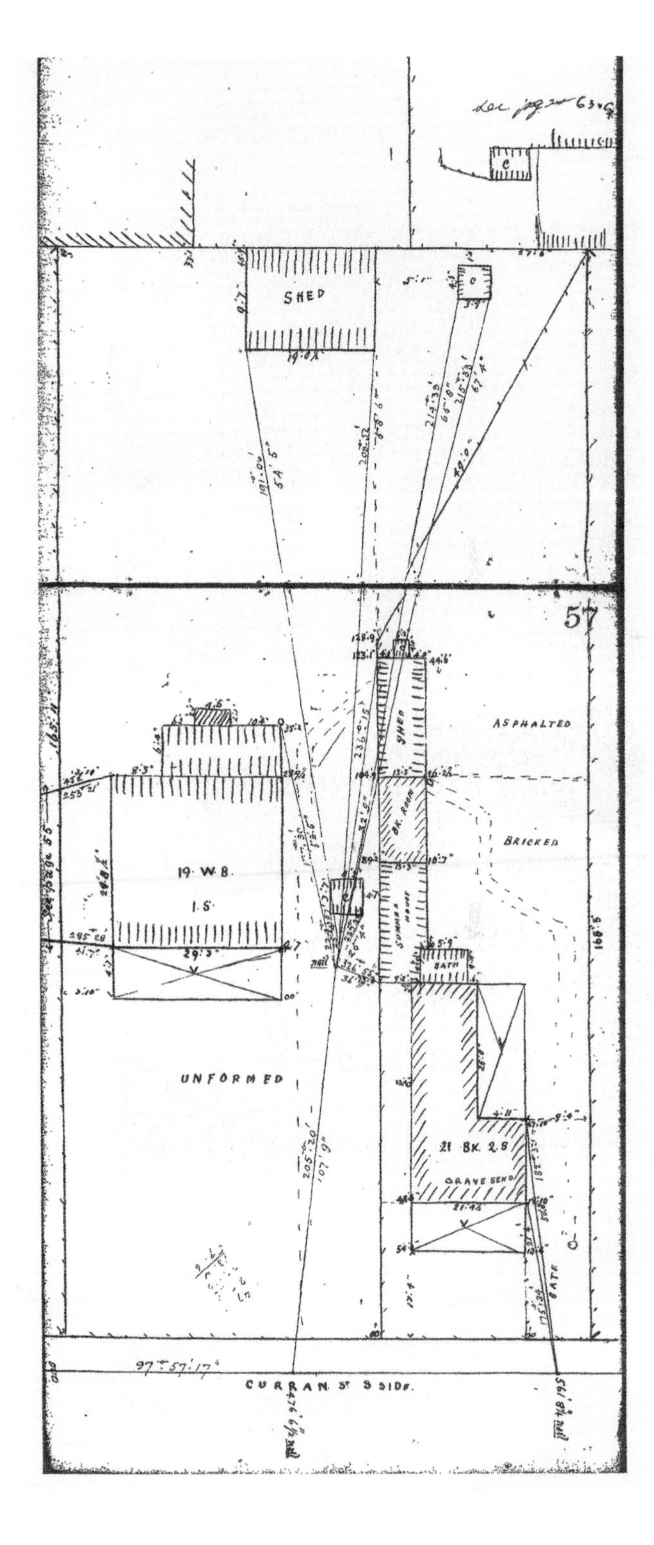

27 Curran Street at bottom was then numbered 21. Number 19 is shown above this.

SOURCE: PROV VPRS 8600, UNIT 24, BOOK 426, PP. 57-58

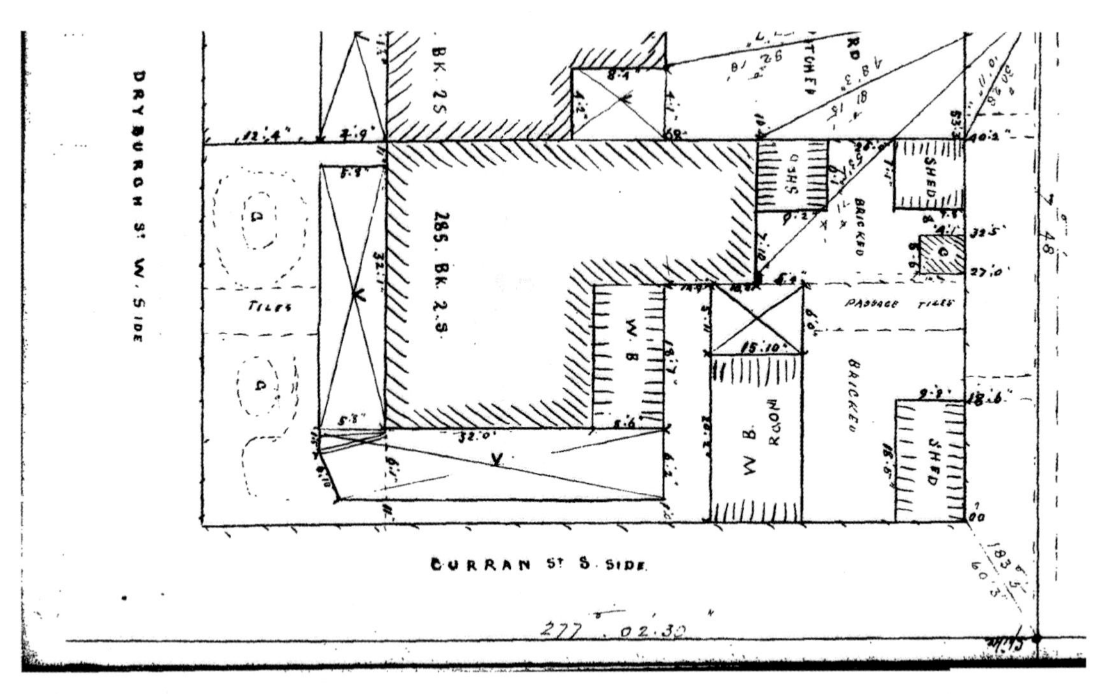

519 Dryburgh Street (then numbered 285).
SOURCE: PROV VPRS 8600, UNIT 24, BOOK 426, PP. 49-50.

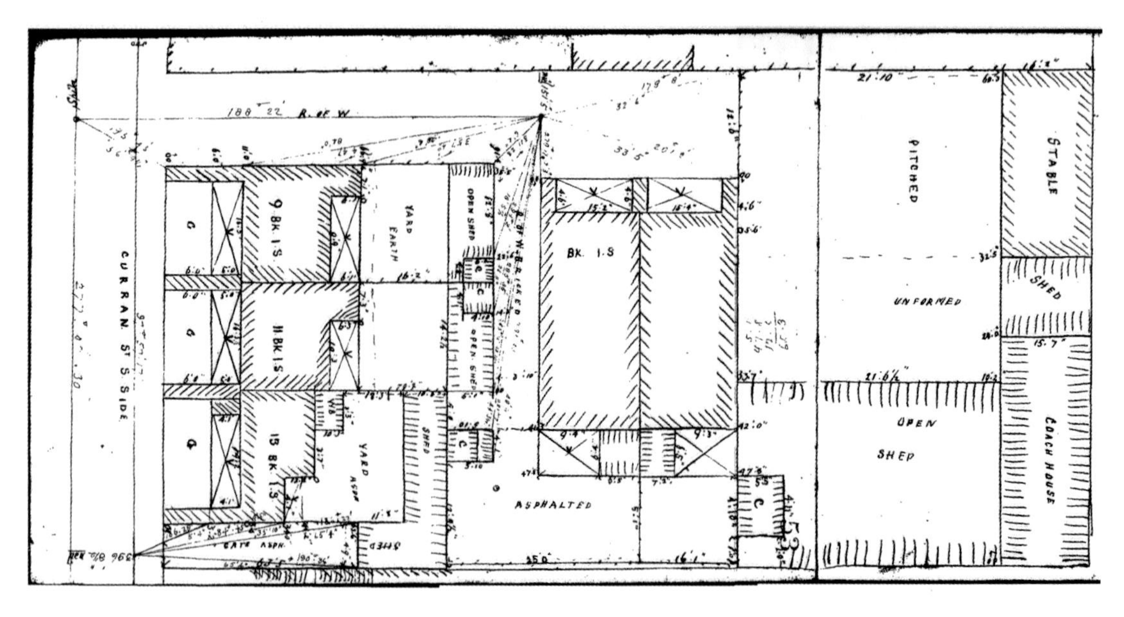

Former Allotment 7 properties.
SOURCE: PROV VPRS 8600, UNIT 24, BOOK 426, PP. 53-54.

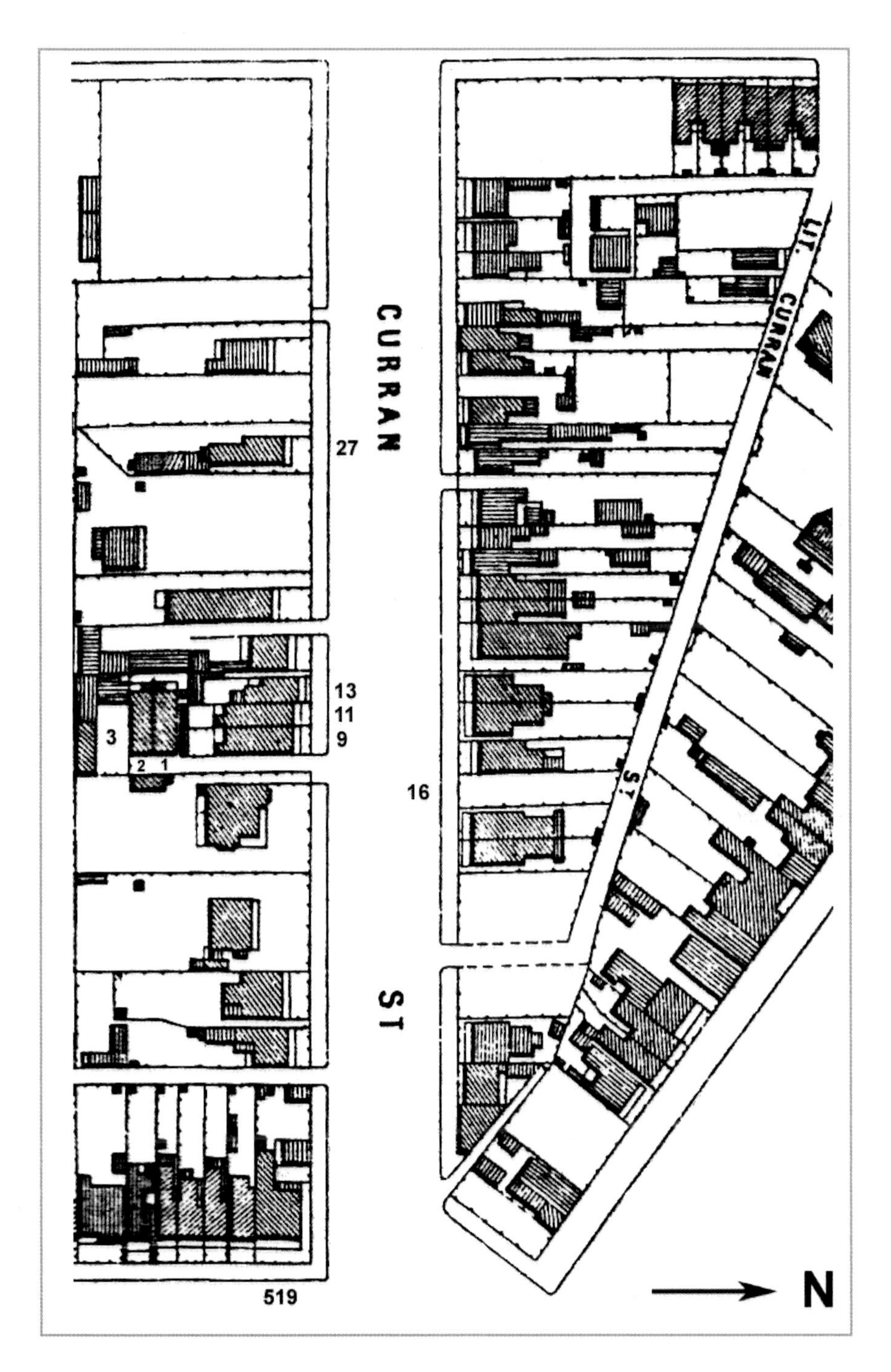

Annotated c.1896 MMBW extract showing the location of the Langford family's Curran Street properties (marked with street numbers). SOURCE: STATE LIBRARY OF VICTORIA.

10
The Land Boomer

Robert's real estate business, R. Langford & Co., kept drawing its proprietor out of Hotham. Sometimes it was because of auctions of country properties. There were trips to see game and seafood suppliers, and new expansion opportunities requiring further investigation. Victoria's population was substantially more decentralised during this period and country centres were relatively more significant as nodes of economic activity. Robert and Elizabeth would also visit relatives and friends in Carisbrook and elsewhere. Robert requested one month's leave from council at the beginning of October 1885 on account of 'important business to transact in Queensland'.[1] He presumably went later in the month, as the *North Melbourne Advertiser* noted that he travelled over 200 miles to attend a dinner at the council chambers on 7 October 1885.[2]

The rounds of social engagements continued up until the end of the year, with a dinner at home for 25 couples in the middle of November. Oysters were served inside the house, while dancing to Bellini's Band continued in a marquee behind the house until 4 am. Robert was briefly ill before Christmas, missing a council meeting. At the end of 1885 work commenced on the new Bible Christian Church around the corner in Brougham Street, built in the same fashionable coloured brickwork as Milton Hall to a design by architect A. E. Duguid.[3] Robert and Elizabeth probably attended the opening service.

Early in December the couple announced their intention to leave the colony for 12 months on a tour of Europe and America. They hoped to depart in March 1886, at which time Robert would retire from council. Milton Hall was for sale. The *Advertiser* reported in late February that it was 'shortly to change hands', but the sale fell through.[4] Robert did, however, sell the Excelsior Auction Rooms to G. A. Stevens soon afterwards.

He and Elizabeth then changed their plans. They liked the country, and were toying with the idea of retiring to Lakes Entrance, where Robert planned to spend

£2500 on buying a large hotel overlooking Reeves River, which they would extend and convert into the Langford's Club Hotel.[5] They said they would take possession of the property on 9 March, but this apparently did not eventuate either.

With Robert and Elizabeth preparing to leave Hotham, 50 guests attended a farewell dinner at Clements Café in Swanston Street on 13 March. The dinner invitations said it was to mark Robert's 'retirement from business', though he quickly pointed out this was not the case. James Pierce chaired the dinner, proposing the health of a man who, in 25 years of acquaintance had shown 'the highest character for honesty and integrity'. Robert was presented with a magnificent framed, illuminated address, measuring 4.5 feet by 3 feet.

> Surrounding the address [were] several well executed sketches, showing the new Princes bridge, the city coat of arms, a tempting lobster, the photo of the recipient, a yacht in full sail, the Hotham Town Hall, the fish market and a scene from the Gippsland Lakes.[6]

Robert said at the dinner he had actually made up his mind to stay at Hotham, but nevertheless later in the year he purchased and moved into an eight-roomed timber house, 'Clyde Bank', in the fashionable eastern suburb of Hawthorn. It may have been planned as a temporary relocation, but the surroundings were pleasant and it was close enough for Robert to easily attend council meetings.

Milton Hall was finally sold to a neighbour and colleague from the fish markets, Percy Jenkins, on 15 March 1887.[7] Jenkins and his wife Mathilda had attended some of Robert's Mayoral functions and their eldest daughter Maud was a guest at Mrs Langford's fancy dress party. Robert retained his other Curran Street properties until the turn of the century.

The proposed move to Gippsland reflected Robert's increasing business interests in the district. In the middle of 1886, he began a bold venture to develop the fishing village of Toorallook into a resort town, Paynesville.

Land speculation could be a fast way of making money. The colony was mid-way through a long, sustained economic boom that lasted until the early 1890s. Land values were constantly rising. In the city, suburbs such as Canterbury, Surrey Hills, Kew, Box Hill, Doncaster, Clifton Hill, Fairfield, Heidelberg, Brunswick, Brighton and Mentone were being laid out or extended. Investors made large profits from subdivisions as new railway lines

The former Bible Christian Church in Brougham Street, completed just before Robert and Elizabeth moved to Hawthorn. Robert was a leading subscriber in the drive to raise funds for its construction. The church is now part of the Abbeyfield elderly accommodation centre. SOURCE: NORTH MELBOURNE LIBRARY.

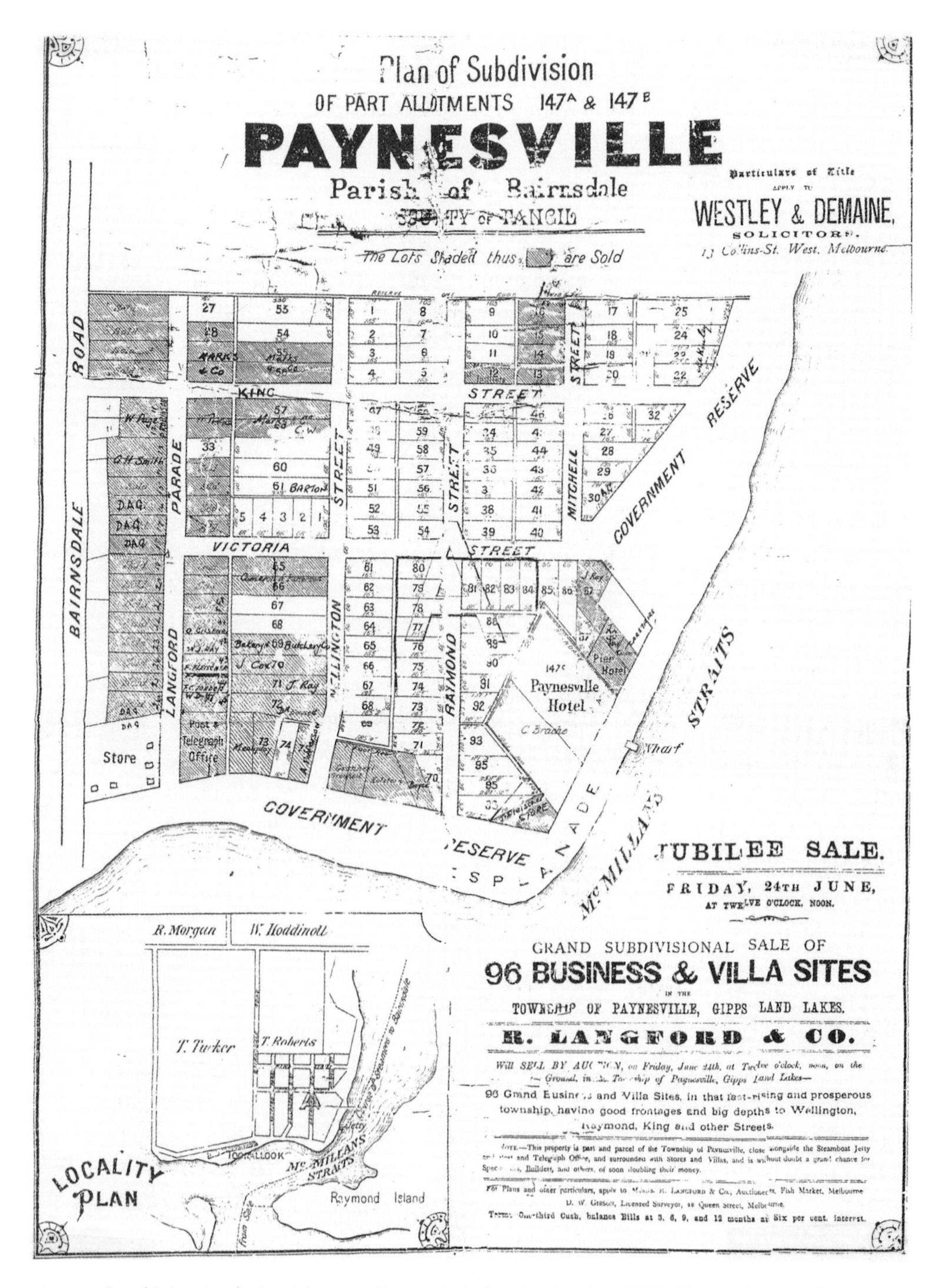

Auction plan of Robert Langford's subdivision at Paynesville, believed to date from 1897. This was the year of Queen Victoria's 60th Jubilee, hence the term 'Jubilee Sale' and the patriotic street names.
SOURCE: EAST GIPPSLAND HISTORICAL SOCIETY

and tram connections snaked their way into these areas. At the peak of the boom, Melbourne real estate was one of the most profitable investments in the country. [8] Certain country areas were also becoming attractive to holiday makers, particularly along the coast, as railway and steamship links made parts of the Victorian coast much more accessible. These were also targeted by speculators.

On 13 June 1886, Robert purchased large sections of what had originally been Crown Allotments 147A and 147B in the Parish of Bairnsdale.[9] This encompassed a large area of land behind the then existing foreshore reserves, which became the centre of the new township. Toorallook was renamed Paynesville in 1888, after the Harbour Master and Inspector of Fisheries, Captain Payne. Langford subdivided the land into 96 business and villa sites, creating a series of new roads including Langford Parade, Wellington Street, Raymond Street, King Street and Victoria Street. Lots were targeted at affluent Melburnians and Gippsland residents for holiday homes. Tourism to the Gippsland area was becoming increasingly popular by the 1880s, helped by the opening of a railway to Sale in 1879. Visitors could catch the train to Sale, then travel on to Paynesville, Bairnsdale or Lakes Entrance by steamer. The Paynesville wharf was on the eastern shoreline in front of the Paynesville and Pier Hotels. A post and telegraph office was opened in 1885. The inland waters of the Lakes were ideal for yachting and other recreational activities.[10]

Robert began auctioning blocks in a long series of sales, including seven over August-September 1886, 14 blocks over 1887, a further 12 in 1888 and three in 1889. Early purchasers of lots included William Mentiplay from the fish markets, and a local fisher family, the Carstairs. Sales slowed significantly with the economic downturn of the 1890s, and never really took off again until after 1910. Nevertheless, the venture began bringing in significant returns within the next few years, and was an intermittent source of income over the coming decades.[11] Over the coming years, Robert gradually bought more allotments, principally suburban land at Nunawading and country allotments around Carisbrook, Talbot, and Bairnsdale.[12]

With the boom Melbourne was coming of age as one of the world's great Victorian cities, like Manchester, Leeds or Birmingham. The low rise, central city was physically transformed. Landmark public buildings were erected or extended and office blocks reached new heights of eight storeys. The massive domes of the new Law Courts (modelled after the Dublin counterpart) and the Exhibition Building (modelled on Brunelleschi's Cathedral in Florence) loomed on a skyline that became dotted with towers, spires and cupolas. Banks and investment houses built grand, classically styled headquarters along Collins Street. With so much construction under way, there were labour shortages in the building industry. The city was increasingly serviced by the most modern infrastructure, cable trams, steam engines, telephones and electric lighting.

Trade at the fish market was also steadily growing. By 1886 it was noted that 'the average fish supply was 10,000 bushels (each 33lb) per month ... The trade had been built up by Mr Langford, by whose exertions the revenue had increased from £300 to £3,000.'[13] Some people called him 'The Fish King' of Melbourne, though with his competitors the title would have been more debatable.

In 1887 Hotham changed its name to the town of North Melbourne. Robert's attendance at council meetings was slipping and he finally decided to resign from both North Melbourne Council and the Hotham Board of Advice in July 1887. A letter in the *Advertiser* explained his action was 'owing to my business calling me away very much in the country, that I find that it is impossible for me to attend as often as I would like at the council table, or the meetings of the Hotham Board of Advice'.[14] His father-in-law William had also resigned from Carisbrook Council on 8 June, midway through his second term, council accepting the resignation 'with regret'.[15]

Robert was continuing to expand his rural interests. In 1889 he acquired 'Beulah' on the Riddell-Sunbury Road, Riddells Creek, in the Sandy Creek Valley outside Romsey. This latter property consisted of a villa and 40 acres of land including orchards. The property had been originally developed and consolidated by George W. Knight, who established vineyards and an orchard, constructing the first house there by the early 1870s. By the time Knight sold the property to Charles Maplestone, the vineyard was producing a substantial output of wine. The house is thought to have been rebuilt by auctioneer Joseph R. Tuckett during the 1880s.[16]

Robert was probably first drawn to Romsey in connection with the growing rabbit trade in the area. R. Langford & Co. later established an agent in Romsey, W. T. Moffat, who undertook clearing sales, and daily auctions of rabbits, poultry, eggs, and other farm and dairy produce. Advertisements for the business appeared in the *Romsey Examiner*.[17]

Back in Curran Street, Robert's mother Harriet died in August 1888. Robert further subdivided 13 Curran Street at about this time, building two small cottages at the rear and turning the former stable driveway into a laneway, Curran Place. His sister Harriet moved into one cottage in 1890 after her husband Charles had deserted her. The particular circumstances of this are unclear. A notice seeking his apprehension appeared in the *Victoria Police Gazette* on 2 April.

> Charles Johnson is charged, on warrant, with deserting his wife Harriet Johnson, at 20 Boundary Road, Hotham Hill, on the 13th instant. Description - Swede, fish hawker, 36 years of age, 5 feet 9 or 10 inches high, thin build, fair complexion, brown hair, sandy moustache and goatee, not whiskers; wore light brown tweed sac coat, brown tweed trousers, and black soft felt hat. He left his wife and three children, stating he was going up country to look for work.[18]

(According to the same source, Charles was apprehended the following month.[19])

Harriet moved from Boundary Road a few blocks away into one of the new houses at 2 Curran Place, where she lived until her death in the 1920s. James and Euphemia were still living around the corner and her father was across the yard at Milton Cottage. Charles was another of a growing list of Robert's relatives working in the fish industry. After attending Scotch College, James's sons Robert and Arthur had joined the family business, Euphemia's brother James Rea also working for the Langfords.[20]

Robert's political ambitions were growing. Success in the council arena encouraged him to look to bigger things.

Elections were being held for the 14th Victorian Parliament in March 1889, and Robert decided to stand as a Liberal candidate. It was common for parliamentarians to began their political careers as local councillors. The five other candidates included his old friends Dr Rose and the incumbent, John Laurens. Robert said he was not out to fight any particular individual. Of those standing, the *Advertiser* characterised Dr Joyce as a 'total Prohibitionist', Mr Murphy 'the working man's candidate, Mr Laurens a Liberal and local optimist, Dr Lloyd an independent Liberal, Mr R. Langford a working man's friend and limited Sunday trading advocate', while Dr Rose contested on 'strong personal grounds, backed up by the North Melbourne Liberal Association'. It was a tall order trying to unseat Laurens, who had held the seat since 1877. He was a serious and dedicated parliamentarian, a Protectionist, who had served on the Royal Commission on banking laws and the westward extension of Melbourne in 1887.[21]

Robert held a big open-air meeting at the Melrose Hotel, around the corner from Curran Street, on 7 March, addressing over 400 people. He described himself as 'not a brilliant speaker' but with 'brains enough to sink a ship'. He had taken out lengthy campaign advertisements explaining his positions.

> Mr Robt. Langford.
> The Labor and advanced Candidate,
>
> IS IN FAVOUR OF
> The Moonee Ponds Creek being constructed and maintained by the Government,
> The Removal of the Benevolent Asylum from its present site,
> The Improvement of the Royal Park,
> The Improvement of the West Melbourne Swamp, and converting the same into docks and Railway Sites,
> Federation for the Colonies, and Protection against the World,
> Limited Hours for Sunday Trading,
> Metropolitan Board of Works, &c,
> Opening the Library and Museums on Sundays, at the same hours of the Zoological Gardens,
> Reduction of Railway Freights on all Farm Produce,
> Railway Extension to Country Towns,

> Irrigation throughout the Agricultural Districts of the Colony,
> Absentee Tax,
> Eight Hours' Movement and Labour Representation.
>
> IS OPPOSED TO
> The Stock Tax,
> The Influx of Chinese,
> The Harbour Trust sending Work out of the Colony, &c.[22]

He was a Liberal candidate sympathetic to workers' rights. The reference to him as a labour candidate is a descriptive not a partisan label, the modern Labor party not formed as a political organisation until the 1890s. Many of the issues raised in his platform had been of concern to him as a councillor, but could only be resolved by the next level of government. The Harbour Trust had commissioned dredges from British suppliers, which he thought should be manufactured locally. He would have met Alfred Deakin, a leading advocate of federation, future Australian Prime Minister and the member for Bourke. In opposing Chinese immigration, Robert's position reflected prevailing social attitudes, though on a personal level he worked with Chinese at the Fish Markets and mixed socially with the Chinese community at Paynesville. He was also 'not in favour of Coalition Government, of Bible reading in State schools ... cutting up the park lands into building allotments, nor of plural voting.' He was in favour of 'Australians having a voice in the election of their own Governor'.[23] He thus was conservative Protectionist, but with a consistent sympathy for workers' rights, perhaps reflecting the hardship he was said to have experienced in his early years.

The polling occurred on Thursday 28 March at the Town Hall and another location in Parkville. Queensberry Street from Leveson to Errol Streets was 'black with waggonette roofs', where an estimated crowd of 10 000 had gathered to hear the result. Smoking a cigar, Robert arrived in a four-horse carriage. Only men were voting, with women not granted the franchise until the early 1900s. Final count was Laurens 864, Murphy 539, Rose 389, Lloyd 331, Langford 197 and Joyce 73.

On hearing the result the candidates and their supporters up on the Town Hall balcony became unruly, showing 'a large amount of personal feeling'. There was a huge roar as John Laurens, then the unsuccessful candidates, addressed the crowd in turn. Robert could not hide his disappointment.

> Fellow electors, although defeated on this occasion, I expected to be treated in a more liberal manner than I have been by my friends, who if they had done as promised, I would have been at the top of the poll. Previous to polling day, in totting up the promises, I found that I had between 700 and 800 pledges, but I feel there must have been some clique at work to upset my calculations ... I cannot congratulate you on placing the old fossil at the head of the poll ... There will be thunderous little good done by him except sitting on the rail.[24]

The result was not that surprising. Laurens was a good representative and Robert was a first-time candidate. He had been a popular Mayor, but one of the less active councillors. His connections with Hotham had lapsed and colonial politics was a much harder game.

On failing to enter the Legislature, Robert stood again for North Melbourne Council early in 1890. A vacancy in the Eastern Ward opened after the death of a sitting councillor, Hugh Wilson, with the election scheduled to take place on 18 February. A key issue was Annexation of the Town of North Melbourne to the City of Melbourne. Advocates of annexation pointed to Melbourne's lower rates and generally better maintenance. There were concerns that North Melbourne was becoming excessively indebted.

Robert stood against the pro-annexation candidate, John Barwise, representing the non-annexation side. He had written to the North Melbourne Liberal Association requesting its support, but a poll of its membership revealed it was in favour of annexation by 2 to 1. Annexation was actually quite popular in the electorate. He had shown poor political judgement. The *Advertiser* was scathing.

> [Mr Robert Langford] has been fooled by a deputation of the CITIZENS to become a candidate ... It seems an inexplicable mystery how Mr Langford as an anti-annexationist could have been asked by the 'citizens' to come from the other side of the Yarra to represent the interests of the ratepayers in the neglected Eastern Ward of the Town of North Melbourne ... [Mr Langford] was present at the council meeting last Monday evening, and was shown marked attention. It seems very much as if he were the nominee of the council ... Mr Langford during the last twelve months he represented North Melbourne was absent the best part of the time and at length resigned, washing his hands of the town until the late Legislative Election when he unsuccessfully contested the seat.[25]

Robert withdrew from the contest, citing 'rumours' as the reason, firing back at the *Advertiser*'s criticisms in his announcement.

> In withdrawing from the present contest I feel that as there are certain rumours abroad that I have been brought forward as the nominee of the Councillors of North Melbourne, and that they are paying my expenses, and as my honour as well as the said Councillors', are at stake, I feel compelled to show the certain parties who have circulated the said lie by withdrawing. I must say that the Councillors of North Melbourne had nothing to do with my entering the present contest, and as a Ratepayer and Property owner of far greater extent than a stable, I had, after several deputations had waited upon me, decided to come forward to contest the vacant seat, from which I now withdraw on account of the unfounded rumours.[26]

Showing resilience, Robert nominated for Healesville Shire Council later in the year. Healesville was a 'pretty municipal township with post, telegraph and money-order

View along Flinders Street from the east of the new Fish Markets, which opened at the western end of Flinders Street in 1890.
SOURCE: STATE LIBRARY OF VICTORIA

office and savings bank' as well as four hotels, five churches and several stores.[27] It had a population of 1200. Even then it was known to Melbourne holiday-makers, who could journey the 60 kilometres east by train. Robert was able to commute from Hawthorn for the monthly meetings, Elizabeth possibly travelling out with him for a few pleasant days away. The area was surrounded by beautiful, heavily timbered ranges, dotted with fern gullies and occasional farms. As with Paynesville, Robert may have been attracted to the area by real estate ventures. It was odd he would make this commitment when he was also setting down roots in Romsey.

The withdrawal of his nomination for North Melbourne Council was somewhat humiliating, but it was typical of Robert to throw his hat in the ring in the first place, and move on to something new when the attempt failed. He had a constant eye out for new opportunities, could accept and manage risk and take a philosophical view if things did not work out as planned.

In 1890 the Fish Market moved to a new red brick building located on a wedge of land between Flinders Street and the Yarra, with one end facing Spencer Street. It was elongated in plan, intersected by a railway overpass, with conical roofs and a Moorish central clock tower where colonies of pigeons settled.[28] It included large refrigerated cool rooms. Refrigeration technology played a critical role in Australia's growing international trade in perishable foodstuffs – frozen fish was routinely imported from New Zealand. Robert and James relocated their business, the old fish market eventually being demolished to make way for the new Flinders Street Railway Station in the 1900s. In about 1891 the brothers also opened a shop at Beach Street, Port Melbourne.

The 1880s was a financially successful period for this ambitious fishmonger turned land auctioneer and property speculator, but dark clouds were looming on the horizon.

11
Romsey and the final years

In the elections of 1889, a new government had been formed under James Munro. Robert's friend John Laurens had returned to Parliament at the beginning of what became an increasingly desperate period. Melbourne was about to experience a severe economic depression.

The economic and property booms of the 1880s and early 1890s had been underpinned by large borrowings of capital from British investors. Their willingness to lend ceased from about early 1891. They had been making excessive large scale investment in outback sheep stations for some years. Many of these were in remote, marginal areas, which were devastated by a drought, causing large losses. Barings, a major London bank, collapsed after defaults by Argentinian borrowers, causing a wave of jitters amongst lenders who then examined their foreign lending policies and concluded that Australia's economic circumstances were not sustainable. Virtually all lending to the Australian private sector abruptly stopped, leading to a net outflow of capital in 1893 and 1894.[1]

The resulting depression affected the country as a whole, though its impact was particularly felt in Melbourne and the consequences were severe. A string of major banks and companies collapsed; companies and banks ceased trading; unemployment rose; Victoria experienced a property market crash. Until 1890, insolvencies in Victoria had averaged around 320 per year. This rose to 445 in that year, 420 in 1891 and 509 in 1892.[2] Prominent individuals who formerly had been amongst the richest men in the city found themselves bankrupt. Residential and commercial construction virtually ceased, leading to a generation of Melbourne architects either to end their careers or emigrate. The economic slump and population stagnation ultimately caused Melbourne to cede to Sydney its position as Australia's most populous city and de facto financial capital. In Australia as a whole real per capita income did not recover to its 1890 level until around 1907.[3]

For anyone in business, these developments brought instability and uncertainty. For individuals involved in property speculation, this meant potentially catastrophic losses. The saleable value of all of Robert Langford's property holdings fell substantially, while the size of debts or mortgages remained the same. The value of his Curran Street properties, for example, fell by a third. He had borrowed heavily to finance many of his property investments, principally from the Commercial Bank of Australia. Financially, things became progressively more difficult financially for Robert over the next few years.

Reflecting the difficult times, weekly rent for a stall at the new fish markets fell from £1-10s-0d in October-December 1892 to £1-5s-0d in January-June 1893.[4] In July of 1894 Jenkins and Langford made representations to council advocating a further reduction in dues, and that they be charged as a percentage of sales rather that fixed rent.[5] Langford and Hill later asked for another reduction at a subsequent visit to the Town Clerk in January 1895, in light of 'alleged falling off in business'.[6] Rent fell to £1-2s-6d in January-March 1896.[7]

Elizabeth's mother Mary died in 1893 and her father William Miller died at Carisbrook the following year. Robert was an executor of his estate, which totalled £138-5s-10d in property and money, including five houses in Carisbrook.[8]

By 1894 Robert and Elizabeth had moved to Romsey to live permanently. They were escaping to the country. They sold 'Clyde Bank' in Hawthorn, and moved to 'Beulah', which they had renovated and renamed 'Rosenberg Park'.[9] It was their most expansive residence yet.

> [Rosenberg is] built in the most substantial manner, and containing 21 rooms, comprising wide hall, dining room (40ft x 15ft), drawing room (927ft 9in x 15ft 10 in), billiard, smoking and sitting rooms, large bedrooms, bathrooms, pantries, kitchens, larder, storerooms, & c; large conservatory. The outbuildings are of a most complete character, comprising laundry, stabling, coachhouses, workshops, & c. The grounds, consisting of about 36 acres, are artistically laid out in lawns, flower, fruit, and vegetable gardens; also paddocks laid down in English grass. There is a plentiful supply of water laid all over the property, and it is situated within 10 minutes walk of the Riddells Creek railway station.[10]
>
> From the Riddells Creek railway the home presents a striking aspect. Its broad frontage, its numerous windows glistening in the sunshine, its two fine balconies, its red roofed stables and outhouses suggest thrift.[11]

Friends in the new locality persuaded Robert to stand for council in the Riddells Creek Riding, when the position of an existing councillor had fallen vacant though non-attendance. He was elected unopposed in early August 1894, attending his first council meeting on 7 September. Cr James Hemphill was Mayor.

As in North Melbourne, the Langfords immersed themselves in community affairs over the next few years. Robert joined the board of the Riddells Creek Waterworks Trust, where he often acted as chairman.[12] He was elected to the Council's Parks Committee, which oversaw the management of the local racecourse and public park[13] and he became a member of the Gisborne Mechanics Institute.[14] He was a steward of the Riddells Creek Racing Club, and patron of the Romsey Amateur Turf Club. A visiting nephew, 'Bobbie' Lewis (son of one of Elizabeth's sisters), rode one of Robert's horses in the local races. (Bobbie later became a celebrated jockey, riding the winner of the 1902 Melbourne Cup.) Robert became president of the local Rosenberg Cricket Club and was Master of Ceremonies at the Cricket Club's concert and ball on 24 May 1895. Mr and Mrs Langford awarded special medals for bowling and batting. Over the next few years, there was much flamboyant hospitality 'under Councillor Langford's mahogany'.

Their interest in the local children continued, Robert joining the school's Board of Advice. On one occasion he and Elizabeth made a surprise visit to Riddells Creek State School.

> The children (numbering nearly 60), attending the Riddells Creek State School, No. 523, had a very pleasant surprise recently ... when Mr Langford, Rosenberg Park (chairman of the Board of Advice) paid a visit to the school. After addressing the scholars in a very appropriate manner, he presented each one with a packet of lollies. It is also worthy of note that a very short time ago, Mrs Langford distributed a basket of oranges amongst the pupils. Three ringing cheers were given for Mr and Mrs Langford, after which the children, thoroughly pleased, departed for their respective homes.[15]

In January 1885, it was announced that Robert and Elizabeth had opened Rosenberg House as a private hotel, which specialised in treating its guests 'to a speciality in fish and game dinners and oyster suppers'. Elizabeth acted as manager and hostess. The *Gisborne Gazette* commented that the district was becoming increasingly popular with holiday-makers, and four guest houses had recently opened in the area. The whole enterprise was almost lost when the chimney on their house next to the main building caught fire on the 8 January, but timely intervention saved the whole complex from burning down. A steady stream of visitors began staying at the property. Guests could play billiards, walk in the gardens and go fishing.[16] They could see a coach builder making a buggy in one of the outbuildings.[17]

It is apparent that conversion of the house to a hotel was motivated by Robert's increasingly acute financial situation. He was experiencing a cash flow crisis, with not enough realisable income from his substantial property holdings to cover ongoing expenses. After a period of increasing difficulty, on 28 June 1895 he finally declared himself insolvent.

The declaration he submitted to the Court of Insolvency outlined his financial position in a series of lists. List A was a catalogue of debts to secured creditors, List B of unsecured creditors, List D of property holdings at the time of the declaration and in the two years previous, List E of stock in trade and personal property (which Robert prudently or deceitfully valued at nil), List F of particulars of all debts owed to him and List H, the names and addresses of, and amounts owing to, all creditors.

Early 20th century view of Rosenberg Park at Riddells Creek, outside Romsey, which Robert and Elizabeth renovated and occupied during the 1890s. Robert served on Romsey Council, and became Mayor in 1896.
SOURCE: SALVATION ARMY ARCHIVES

Robert owed creditors £12 283-2s-9d while the value of money owed to him and his property holding came to only £9570, leaving a deficit of £2710-12s-9d. This exposure may be entirely attributed to the decline in property values that occurred after 1891, which would have transformed what would have been a very healthy ledger before that time.[18]

The list of Robert's debtors and creditors provides a snapshot of his business relationships and lifestyle at the time, with outstanding debts to 60 companies and individuals. Most of his real estate holdings were mortgaged, his single biggest creditor being the Commercial Bank of Australia, which had lent him £4102 in September 1892. Other credit institutions he owed were the Australasian Temperance and General Mutual Life Assurance Society Limited (owed £256), the Modern Permanent Building and Investment Society (owed £78-7s-6d) and the Standard Mutual Building Society (owed £55).

A mortgage of £2383 was due to oyster merchant James Radford Allen, with debts relating to the Fish Market business, including small sums due to carters, warehousemen and newspaper offices for advertising services. There were outstanding living expenses, with bills due to a wine merchant, hotel keeper, plumber, baker, timber merchant, blacksmith, saddler, grocer, butcher and nurseryman. Their old friend, Dr J. M. Rose of Collins Street, Melbourne was owed £8-10s for medical consultations in 1892, and a Dr Daly in Gisborne was owed £5-5s for medical services provided in August 1894. An undertaker in Bairnsdale was owed 15s for services provided in 1893, possibly for the funeral of Elizabeth's mother. Their servant at Riddells Creek, Thomas Randolph Cosman, was owed £81 for 11 months' wages. Money was also owed to members of Robert's immediate family. There was a mortgage of £1271 on the Curran Street properties due to his brother James, £49 owed in wages to his other brother John Richard Langford for work done as a servant, and £15 due to his father John.[19]

Robert in turn was owed the smaller amount of £1838-7s-3d by 63 individuals, most of which was listed as bad or doubtful debt. In compiling these (List F), Robert appears to have done a comprehensive audit of his business records to identify all outstanding monies from the last decade and before, with the oldest debt listed being for about £4 owed by a fisherman in Echuca since 1883. Most of the debtors were fishermen, typically for small amounts due for fish stock sold or money left, this debtors list indentifying many of the fishmarket business's regional suppliers. There was £200 in bad debts owed by G. A. Stevens of York, Western Australia, presumably the same individual to whom Robert had sold the Excelsior Auction Rooms in 1886. Interestingly, the architect George Raymond Johnson, designer of the Hotham Town Hall and possible architect of Milton Hall, owed Robert £79-16s-2d, which was written off as a bad debt.[20]

Robert certainly owed a lot of money, but presumably it was not all due at once. There was also always the possibility that the cash flow crisis and his negative net worth might be ameliorated by a recovery in land prices and some successful large sales.

The insolvency was publicly known, with a notice announcing the statutory meeting of creditors required by law appearing in the *Gisborne Gazette* in July 1895. Robert's largest creditors (those owed more than £25) were to attend and determine a schedule for repayments by vote. The meeting was called at the Collins Street offices of solicitor Frank Martin Russell on 5 July, but this was adjourned to 12 July. Ten debtors (or their proxies), representing £4881-18s-2d in debt, attended the rescheduled meeting. Agreement was made to settle the debt with a payment of just 1s-6d in the pound, to be paid in instalments over the next 12 months.[21]

It would seem extraordinary that Robert be relieved of this debt so generously, but this was not an unusual outcome for a creditors meeting. Victorian law at this time allowed three-quarters of the creditors (by value and number) at a meeting to vote on a settlement rate which would then be applied to all outstanding debts. It was well known that creditors meetings could be manipulated towards a more favourable outcome for the insolvent by the presence of friends and family members in order to gain the three-quarters vote.[22] Those voting for the 1s 6d in the £ solution for Robert's debts included two of his brothers, and friends such as Cr Somerville from Romsey. Robert may have entered into private arrangements with other creditors for more time. He was not required to immediately transfer any of his assets, or sell personal effects, having listed his personal property as valued nil. Selling all his properties was not going to balance all his debts in any case, although he sold some land in Carisbrook for £400 in October and sold the rest of his holdings there in 1898.[23]

Events must have been distressing, but over time it was manageable. He took a total of three months leave of absence from council spread out over four periods for 'business reasons'.[24] An article in the *Romsey Examiner* on October suggested Robert was in arrears for rates, which he denied. R. Langford & Co. went on trading at the Melbourne fish markets. Meanwhile Robert continued with council and various community interests. He did not refrain from dreaming up new business schemes either.

One of Robert's more exotic business proposals was to manufacture a snakebite antidote commercially. Snakes were common around Riddells Creek. A visiting snake expert, a Professor Davies, spent some time at Rosenberg House in August 1885.[25] He was there in connection with some tests Robert was carrying out on an antidote formula, which he had been given in Gippsland several years previously by the late Mr Shires, a well-known snake charmer. Some snakes captured from the Royal Park Gardens were specially brought in. Tests were carried out on dogs, with varying success. There was a suggestion that when the weather warmed up and more snakes came out of hibernation, Robert would give a public demonstration of the potion.[26]

When the vacant council seat Robert had filled in 1894 was up for re-election in August 1895, he was returned, once again unopposed. Cr Peter Mitchell was elected Mayor at the next council meeting on 4 October 1895 and retiring Mayor James Hemphill was presented with a customary illuminated address at a special function held at the Commercial Hotel. After the speeches the party moved to the adjoining dining room where Robert provided a sumptuous fish dinner for all those present, the menu including fried Murray cod and oysters in the shell, specially prepared and sent over by Mrs Langford.[27]

As he grew older Robert began having eye problems and he came down with a particularly bad eye infection in late November/early December of 1896.[28] Photographs show him wearing small, rounded spectacles from his forties onwards. The *Romsey Examiner* satirised the ailing Romsey councillors in August 1896.

> In some respects the Romsey council chamber on Friday resembled the casualty ward at the Melbourne Hospital. Cr Somerville came in on a stick – not riding it as little boys do, but leaning on it heavily, for he had had an attack of the gout, and was unable to put one of his feet to the ground. Cr Langford's eyes were hidden behind spectacles, and he appeared able to see only with great difficulty, and Cr Baker, who is not as 'spry' as he used to be, was walking lame through an old leg trouble which seems to stick to him like a pitch plaster. Under all the circumstances it was very good of these gentlemen to turn up. Crs Somerville and Langford said they would not have done so only it was Cr Mitchell's last meeting.[29]

Robert brought a sense of humour to council meetings, although some people said he was 'not beyond a few crude ways' as he became older.

> Cr Maxted said a dead goose had been lying on the road near Romsey for several days, and was a source of danger, as it frightened horses. The inspector said the goose was nothing but bones, and the township dogs carried it about from place to place. He recognised it as his duty to bury dead dogs and cats, but had nothing to do with dead wild geese. Cr Langford suggested that this particular feathered bipod was perhaps the township one for raffling purposes.[30]

The Langfords would have known their neighbours, the Amess family. Samuel Amess was a prominent Scottish-born Melbourne builder, who later became a Melbourne City councillor and Mayor. He was on the MCC Markets Committee. He had purchased allotments in the Riddells Creek area including land adjacent to G. W. Knight's original holdings in 1865. His son John continued farming near Riddells Creek in the 1890s, while Samuel retired to his property on Churchill Island in Western Port Bay.[31] Sir William Clarke was also a significant landowner in the district, and supporter of many local activities.

A falling meteor brilliantly lit up the sky over Romsey in the evening of 19 June 1896. The same day, Robert's father John, who had been ill for some time, died in North Melbourne aged 79. His death was mentioned in the *Gisborne Gazette*. In their old age, Robert's parents would have been able to feel their decision to emigrate had been a good one.

Peter Mitchell's year as Mayor came to an end in August 1896, and at the next Council meeting on 16 August members' minds turned to choosing his successor. Cr Maxted nominated Robert Langford, which Cr Hemphill seconded. 'Cr Langford said he greatly appreciated the high honour which his colleagues had bestowed on him ... It was not the first time he had presided over a municipal council, as he had been mayor of North Melbourne, and he trusted that his experience in that municipality would come to his aid now in the important duties which had been entrusted to him.' The Romsey Mayor's allowance of £20 per year reflected the lean economic times, modest in comparison with the North Melbourne stipend of £100.[32] The customary retiring Mayor's dinner was held after the meeting.

Robert requested that council meetings be held on the last Monday of each month, when it was easier for him to get away from his business. Upon becoming Mayor, he was also sworn in as a Justice of the Peace again, perhaps a little unusual for someone who had been declared an insolvent. His first official event as Mayor was on a tour by the Romsey Council of the Metropolitan Farm at Werribee, a massive area of irrigated pastures being established alongside Port Phillip Bay to disperse the effluent from Melbourne's new reticulated sewerage disposal system, still under construction.[33]

A false rumour in late October that the Langfords were about to move to Coolgardie in Western Australia led to Robert publicly correcting the error, announcing he was in fact moving to Bendigo, where he had purchased a business that required his supervision.[34] He intended to continue as Mayor, travelling over for each meeting. Municipal voters rolls list Robert Langford, fishmonger, as living at a house in Myers Street, Bendigo, in 1897-98 and 1898-99, suggesting he moved in early 1897. A farewell dance and social night were held on 30 October, at which Robert was presented with an illuminated address by Cr Somerville. (He must have had a collection of them by now.)

Rosenberg Park was closing down. 'Mrs Langford had received quite a shoal of letters from previous visitors at "Rosenberg" which were highly complimentary, requesting her to reconsider her intention of leaving, and continue to receive visitors during the coming season ... but they could not do so.'[35] Rosenberg was put to auction on 11 November 1896, but failed to meet the reserve price.[36] Robert eventually sold it to the Salvation Army for use as a girls home in 1899.[37] (It is now a private residence, Wychwood House.) The clearing sale of the house and farm contents fared better. Twenty rooms of furniture and effects, horses, ponies, cows, farm implements, buggies, etc. were put to auction at 10.30 am on 23 November 1886, attracting bidders from around the district. Everything was sold except for two ponies and a buggy.[38] Once relocated to Bendigo, Robert travelled across for meetings by train.

Robert Langford, c.1903.
SOURCE: IPHOTOGRAPH COURTESY KAYE CARR.

Robert's failure to enter the Legislature in the previous decade did not dampen his interest in big-picture political issues. He requested that a meeting be held to stimulate local interest in the upcoming Federal Convention election. Candidates were to be elected who would write the constitution for the new Federation of Australia. A Mr William Wilson chaired a meeting of around 30, mainly farmers, at the Mechanics Institute on 3 March. Ten candidates were chosen from those present, whose merits were then debated. 'Cr Thorburn expressed his disappointment with the meeting, as he had expected to hear the principles of federation discussed, and some information given as to how it would affect the colonies; also a summary of the candidates' views.'[39] At least community debate had been kindled.

When Sir William Clarke died on 15 May, council sent a condolence letter to his widow, Lady Janet Clarke. Despite absorbing losses accrued through his share in the troubled

Colonial Bank of Australia, Clarke left an estate of over £1 million, his funeral one of the largest held in Victoria. In the meeting, Robert stated he had known Sir William for over 30 years, but they were more likely acquaintances rather than close friends.[40]

In 1897, as Queen Victoria celebrated her 60th year on the throne, the *Romsey Examiner* published a special Diamond Jubilee supplement to mark the occasion. Robert called a meeting in Romsey Shire Hall to discuss what form the local celebrations might take. Council proposed to help finance a new infectious diseases ward at Kyneton Hospital as a permanent form of commemoration, but ideas were sought for some kind of community event. In the end, a public picnic in Romsey was decided on.[41]

James Langford (left) with three of his five sons.
SOURCE: PHOTOGRAPH COURTESY DIANE MCDONALD

The entire town joined the celebrations on the 23 June. The Lancefield brass band began playing soon after it arrived later on in the afternoon. As the evening sky darkened, coloured lights and illuminated transparencies came on the length of a great sweep of buildings along the main street. At half past six a colossal bonfire was lit on the green behind the Shire Hall, illuminating the sky and surrounding town for half a mile around, and watched by a crowd of 600. After a chorus of 'God Save the Queen' and the firing of a Royal Salute of 60 guns, refreshments were served. Mayor Langford was regretfully unable to attend the celebrations because of business in Bendigo, but hoped the townsfolk would appreciate a large donation of free fried fish. Three hundred battered half-pound pieces were consumed, as well as 7500 sandwiches, bread with cheese and Chelsea buns. The night ended with a display of fireworks.[42]

Robert's year as Mayor came to an end in August, with councillor John Myles Thorburn voted his successor. The last council event was the retiring President's Dinner, held at the Commercial Hotel as usual. It was a men only affair, the tables specially decorated with daffodils from one of the local nurseries and much alcohol apparently consumed. There were toasts to the Queen, the Governor, and the Parliament of Victoria, and the singing of the national anthem. Councillor Langford proposed to the new President, who responded with a toast to the retiring one. Robert regretted having to move away from Romsey. 'Now they wanted him in the council at Bendigo' but 'private affairs, however, did not permit of his accepting any more public responsibilities at present, and he did not intend to remain in Bendigo all his life'.[43]

Elizabeth's brother-in-law Alexander McDonald started a job in a mine at Elmore outside Bendigo in 1898, but after only six weeks was killed in a mining accident, leaving her sister Louise widowed at age 38, with 21 children. Robert and Elizabeth possibly helped to arrange the funeral and provided financial assistance. Louise trained as a mid-wife, and began a long career in which she helped deliver more than 6000 children in Richmond alone.[44] James Langford's wife Euphemia died in 1899. James later married his sister-in-law, Alice Rea.

WEDNESDAY, OCTOBER 17.
At Three O'Clock. On the Premises,
Nos. 9, 11, and 13 CURRAN-STREET,
NORTH MELBOURNE.

FIVE SPLENDID BRICK COTTAGES,
Also, Extensive Stabling and Covered-in Yard, on
Land 66 x 165, on Crown of Hill.

To Cartage Contractors, Investors, and Others.

SYDNEY C. ARNOLD and Co. will SELL by PUBLIC AUCTION, as above, LAND, having a frontage of 66ft. to Curran-street, North Melbourne, upon which are erected 3 substantially-built 5-roomed cottages, producing £96 per annum; and, at rear, substantial stabling and large covered-in yard; also 2 good 3-roomed brick cottages, rental £56.

This property is in thorough repair, and is for positive sale, and is suitable for an investment, or a rare opportunity for a cartage contractor to secure a bargain. No expense has been spared in stabling, and it is ready to walk into.

Title, Certificate.

Robert Langford sold his remaining Curran Street properties in 1900 to confectioner Alfred W. Allen.
SOURCE: *ARGUS*

After a few years in Bendigo, Robert and Elizabeth returned to Melbourne, living in South Melbourne, then purchasing a house at 7 Waltham Street, Flemington in about 1901. Although this was their Melbourne address, they seem still to have spent a substantial amount of time in country Victoria over the next few years. Robert also owned a small timber house across the creek in George Street, North Melbourne, for a period. In October 1900, he sold his remaining Curran Street properties to the confectioner Alfred W. Allen, founder of Allens Sweets.

Through the later years of the 1890s, Robert continued to operate at the fish markets. The Langford brothers were mentioned in the Council Market Committee minutes mainly in connection with routine maintenance issues and occasional disputes. For example, the dividing rail between the Langford and Hill stalls gave way and needed repair in August 1894. The following year Robert complained about receiving from the coolrooms some fish that had gone off, and James had a dispute with the Committee over the payment of dues on some hares in 1898.[45] Robert wrote to the committee on behalf of all the fish salesmen in 1899 drawing attention to the need for the window and door frames at the fish market offices to be repainted. Meanwhile, the markets remained a male-dominated industry. In 1899 the Inspector went so far as to suggest that 'sanitary accommodation for females' be installed at the market.[46]

Like most of the Australian population at the time, Robert considered himself 'a Britisher'. Australians saw themselves as foremost amongst the British Empire's southern representatives. The Federation movement had gathered momentum through the 1890s and after a series of conventions and referendums in the late 1890s, on January 1 1901 the Australian colonies were formally united into a single nation within the British Empire. Edmund Barton became first Prime Minister, the former colonies becoming states whose governments continued to administer lands, railways, roads, schools and industrial matters. The notion of Australian identity was more a legal fact at first, something which the community grew into over time in light of existing stronger identification with Britain or their local state. The death of Queen Victoria on 22 January 1901, after a reign which had begun before the founding of Melbourne itself, further marked a decisive break to a new era.[47]

A photograph survives of Robert pictured with the 'The Curran Street Troopers', a group of local children who collected money to support Australian troops fighting at the Boer War in South Africa. It communicates both 'Uncle' Robert's interest in the local youngsters, but also tells much about the political outlook and identity of Australians at the time, with the cause, the kilts and the Union Jacks.

Needing to stay busy, Robert stood for the Flemington and Kensington Borough Council in August 1902. He gave a good campaign speech at the Centennial Hotel in Kensington, which was reported in detail in the local press. Langford, it was written, was a 'hero of a hundred fights'. This time he supported minimum wage rates for municipal works, extending electric lighting through the main streets, a new ramp at Newmarket Railway Station, landscaping of the Recreational Reserve, the purchase of another water cart to suppress the 'dust fiend' and the repair of roads and footpaths. It was another election with a 'lack of any burning question'. 'If elected as one of their three [new] representatives he would feel as proud of their victory as Lord Kitchener did of his South African Laurels, and if "licked" he would take his defeat in good part.'[48] He was elected.

It was a return to the territory of 20 years earlier. In 1882 he had participated in joint committees between Hotham and Flemington Councils dealing with the Moonee Ponds Creek and West Melbourne Swamp. This time he was representing the other side of the boundary. North Melbourne Council itself ceased to exist after 1905 when

Robert Langford (far right) with 'The Curran Street Troop', local children who collected donations for the Boer War. Robert's nephew George Langford is second from left, wearing a kilt, while another nephew Walter Langford is on the pony.

SOURCE: PHOTOGRAPH COURTESY JOAN SNEDDON.

it was incorporated with the Hopetoun Ward of the City of Melbourne. Robert chose not to stand for re-election in August 1905 as the old tensions between country and city living, and the demands of business, had re-emerged. 'Living as he did at present 63 miles from Melbourne, he had been of late unable to attend the Council as well as he could have wished, and felt like a schoolboy who had been playing truant.'[49]

The business association with his brother in R. & J. W. Langford & Co. continued. Robert was still making the occasional interstate business trip, visiting Brisbane in October 1902.[50] He wrote to the Market Committee in 1903, requesting a reduction in the amount of cold storage space allocated to his firm, and that storage charges be reduced.[51] A profile of Robert including a photograph appeared in the publication, *The Cyclopedia of Victoria*.

Robert's sister Mrs Harriet Johnson (nee Langford) in old age. For many years she and her children occupied a cottage built by Robert at 2 Curran Place.

SOURCE: PHOTOGRAPH COURTESY ROBYN LORENZ.

Robert is not listed in Melbourne directories between 1906 and 1910, suggesting he and Elizabeth again moved to the country or possibly even travelled abroad during these years. They may have moved to the west for a few years to help his nephew Arthur Langford establish a new business. Arthur had worked in the Melbourne business for some years before migrating to Western Australia where he started trading at the Perth Fish Market in about 1908.[52] He was later also listed as a general auctioneer. (Arthur's company A. J. Langford's Fish Merchants is still trading under that name today.)

The titles of some of Robert's remaining 1890s land holdings were transferred to the Commercial Bank of Australia in 1905 and 1909, with ownership of some land he jointly held with a Mr Harry Kosken and Rachel Cooper in Mulgrave being passed to the Mulgrave Shire Council in February 1911 due to non-payment of rates.

R. & J. W. Langford continued trading at the Flinders Street Fish Markets together until shortly before James's sudden death at home on 11 March 1911. After nearly three decades in business together, their partnership was finally over. It is not clear how deep Robert's involvement in the business was in the final decade, in light of his activities in the country, and the employment of James's sons Robert and Arthur, and brother-in-law James Rea in the business. James's son Robert (junior) administered James's estate, which came to £2173-1s, and included the house at 27 Curran Street, an additional vacant allotment in Curran Street and in Somerville Street, Yarraville, two horses, a cart, furniture, baskets and scoops, and a £583-6s-8d interest in his deceased wife Euphemia's personal estate.[53] Robert (junior) was living at 231 Dryburgh Street (now number 465) by this time.

In June, the younger Robert's application to take over his father's market stands (2 and 3) was approved. In May 1912, the markets committee was informed that the Langfords' business had been sold to their former rival Messrs Hill and Son, but this was promptly withdrawn in a letter submitted the following month. Another of James's sons, George, worked at the firm for a few years. It was finally sold by early 1914.[54] With almost a 50-year presence at the markets, Robert had been one of the longest continuous tenants of the Melbourne City Corporation. In August 1914, news came through from Cooma in New South Wales that Robert's other brother John Richard had also died.

Perhaps the older Robert's decision to withdraw from the business was also prompted by declining health. He was still involved in property sales, however, making what was to be his last land sale in the Paynesville development on 29 April, 1915. He and Elizabeth were living at Bay Street, Port Melbourne, when he died of peritonitis on 18 October 1915. He was 66 and he and Elizabeth had been married for 43 years. His death notice appeared in *The Age* the next day.

> Langford, On the 18th of October at the Melbourne Hospital, Robert Langford of 371 Bay Street, Port Melbourne, ex-mayor of North Melbourne, the beloved husband of Lizzie Langford, beloved brother of Mrs Johnson of Curran Street, North Melbourne, aged 66 years.

The funeral went from Bay Street to Coburg Cemetery where he was buried two days later.

'Trifle not, your time's but short' read an inscription at Milton Church in Kent. Robert's three great talents had been business, civic affairs and entertaining. He was a 'self made man', who, like so many others coming from the other side of the world, had some 'very rough experiences' in his early years. Although not highly educated, he had a strong entrepreneurial flair. His commercial interests were balanced with an enjoyment of good living and great generosity. He had been a market trader for 50 years, reflecting his reputation for energy and perseverance. His principal disappointments were most likely his and Elizabeth's childlessness, insolvency and his failure to enter the colonial parliament. The political 'hero of a hundred fights' remained good-natured, with a strong sense of fairness. As a councillor in four localities, he was never voted out of office. The rigorous lifestyle of the market and his love of sport suggest great physical robustness and stamina.

Of his achievements, it was his year as Mayor of Hotham that Elizabeth recalled in his death notice.

∽

Robert did not leave a will.[55] It is thus very difficult to assess his financial standing at the time of his death. Their house in Port Melbourne was by no means an extravagant mansion. It is not known what other properties he still owned by this time. Having recently sold the business, he would have presumably have had some cash savings.

Elizabeth had her own connections in Melbourne. Her sister, Louise, still lived in Richmond and some of Robert's family remained at Curran Street. Old 'Aunty Lizzie' had dozens of nephews and nieces living around the city. For a change of scene, the widowed Elizabeth moved to a house near the Baptist Church in Aberdeen Street, Geelong, where she is recorded as the occupant of number 11 (later renumbered 17) in 1915 and 1916, which she did not own. This was a boarding house, 'Corelba', and although she remarried in 1917, she was listed there as a 'boarding house keeper' until 1918.[56] If she was working from necessity, Robert's estate must have dwindled. Her new husband, Thomas Henry Matthews, had been a driver by occupation – she told the registrar she was 49, not 62. They lived for a few years in Fitzroy until Thomas died in 1921. Elizabeth subsequently married William Henry Augustus Neville in 1923. He was a retired 77-year-old builder from Seaholme, near Altona, and it was his fourth marriage. She became stepmother to three adult children.

The couple were admitted to the Cheltenham Benevolent Asylum on 5 February 1930. This was actually the old Hotham Benevolent Asylum, which had moved to parkland several kilometres from Cheltenham Railway Station in 1911.[57] It still functioned as a charitable institution, but also had special services offering care for the elderly. A condition of entry was that patients leave their property to the asylum. William died a month later, leaving an estate of £658, including land and cottages in High Street, Coburg and at Seaholme. Elizabeth died in December 1931 and was buried with William in the old Cheltenham Cemetery.

Less is know about Elizabeth than about her first husband. She was not profiled by the media and no photographs of her were published. The limited picture of the Mayoress that emerges from the *North Melbourne Advertiser* and the *Romsey Advertiser* is of a capable hostess, and manager, always doting on the local children. As a 17-year-old newlywed, she could not have predicted that she would die alone in the institution that had dominated the suburb where she began married life.

Neither Robert nor Elizabeth has a gravestone, but their time in North Melbourne is recorded in the *North Melbourne Advertiser*, the streets named after them and in the houses they built along Curran Street.

12
Park View 1887–2004

The history of Milton Hall since its sale by the Langfords is a story of successive households and of physical change. The sequence of subsequent owners and occupants is as follows.[1]

Period	*Owner*	*Occupants*
1879–87	Robert Langford	Self
1886–1901	Percy Jenkins	Jenkins family, then tenants 1899–1901
1901–11	Bank of Victoria	Thomas Pitt
1912–23	Edward Mylrea	Mylrea family, tenants
1923–38 1939–46 1946–49	Charles Ringrose Elizabeth Ringrose Reginald Ringrose	Ringrose family & boarders
1947–50	John & Lillian Ross	Not known
1950–68	Margot Pretty	Proprietor & boarders
1969–present	Hugh O'Neill	O'Neill family

Occupancy and physical change

As previously noted, architecturally and technologically, this property represents a typical example of a common inner-Melbourne building type. Consideration of the nature and causes of its physical development sheds light on broader trends and forces at work on the housing stock within the suburb and city as a whole.

On the following pages are biographical sketches of these owners in chronological order, with an account of physical changes made during each period of occupancy. Changes have been compiled using physical evidence, photographs, Melbourne City Council and MMBW records, and personal communications with past occupants. The most substantial have consisted of the addition of a rear wing, construction of internal partitioning to create apartments (and the removal of this), and the construction and removal of various outbuildings. Langford's original house remains essentially intact.

Apart from its social interest, biographical detail of occupants can identify links between personal circumstances and the physical changes to the building. The built environment is the high tide mark of the economic cycle. Wider economic conditions have been an important influence on ownership and occupancy, and physical development. The house was built by a prospering merchant and real estate auctioneer riding the long land boom of the 1880s, a man who could afford to spend money on exuberant decoration and a lookout tower. Financial difficulties led the next owner to lease it out at the end of the 1890s, the title transferring to the Bank of Victoria after his death. Economic depression in the 1930s led to the house being converted into apartments, the building becoming an income-generating asset within a business. This pattern continued until the late 1960s, when it was converted back into a single residence. Boarding houses have become uncommon in the area as the suburb has become increasingly gentrified.

Modernisation has also driven physical change. Since Langford's era, electricity, telephone services, and reticulated sewerage have been introduced, with gas lighting being superseded and wood/coal heating falling from favour. Gas light fittings have been replaced with electric. There have been associated changes in lifestyle. The modern indoor bathroom as a standard feature in Australian homes was still some decades away in 1880. This comfort had been installed beneath the back verandah by the 1920s, and an indoor WC was installed during 1957. Washing is no longer done in a wood-heated copper pot. Machines and labour economics have eliminated the servant from modern middle class households, and the corresponding spatial divisions between servants and employers' domains. In the 19th century, when horses were a principal form of transport, occupants of this house used stable facilities on nearby neighbouring properties. By the 1940s, when motor cars had come into widespread use, a double garage had been built at the rear of the house facing on to Langford's Lane.

Building technology and typology also influence physical change. Light timber structures are much more susceptible to physical decay and fire than masonry. Langford's lookout tower has thus not survived, and timber outbuildings in the rear yard were burnt down in the 1960s. The enclosure of verandahs is a common and economical way to creating additional internal space in a building. With this house the entire first floor verandah was enclosed to create kitchen and bathroom spaces when the building was converted into a boarding house. Back yards are a valued feature of Australian suburban life for their inherently flexible capacity to accommodate different activities. The rear yard of 519 Dryburgh Street has variously contained gardens, a workshop, garage, toilets and a sleepout. Paths and entry points have changed. All garden plantings are essentially transient, and on a site poorly suited to large trees, no pre-1960s vegetation now remains.

Conjectural consecutive plans showing the physical development of the house from c.1882 to the present day. Interior spaces are shown shaded.

Owners 1886-1900

Biographical notes

Percy Jenkins
SOURCE: PHOTOGRAPH COURTESY ROBERT CANNON.

Percy Northumberland Jenkins was born at sea on the *Northumberland* en route to Australia from London in 1854. His father Joseph was a carver, gilder and fishmonger. Percy married Matilda Franks at St John's Church in Melbourne in 1877 and the couple had five children by the time they acquired Milton Hall – Maude, Edith, Percy, Joseph and Ethel. A sixth child, Elsie, arrived in 1888. His sons attended Scotch College.

Jenkins had already been living in the Hotham Hill neighbourhood for several years. By 1882/83 he owned a six-roomed brick cottage along Flemington Road, between Dryburgh and Melrose Streets. He moved then into in one of the two 'Park View' terraces (now 485 and 487 Dryburgh Street) on their completion in 1884. At around the same time he acquired other properties on the opposite corner of

View north along Swanston Street from Flinders Street in 1900. Percy Jenkins's fish shop is visible behind the cart at far left, with a semi-circular sign on the first floor facade (which was illuminated). SOURCE: STATE LIBRARY OF VICTORIA.

UNDER THE PATRONAGE OF
His Excellency the Governor.
HOTELS & FAMILIES SUPPLIED
AT LOWEST MARKET PRICES.
FISH CLEANED & DELIVERED
IN ALL PARTS OF TOWN & SUBURBS.

MELBOURNE FISH & POULTRY DEPOT
P. N. JENKINS
FISHMONGER & POULTERER

A REGULAR SUPPLY OF
MURRAY COD
HOBART TOWN TRUMPETER
OYSTERS, CRAYFISH &c.
THE CHOICEST KINDS OF SMOKED FISH
ALWAYS ON HAND
5, SWANSTON STREET.
& FISH MARKET.
MELBOURNE

Mr Johnson Nov 1st 1883

Bought of P. N. Jenkins.
WHOLESALE & RETAIL
FISHMONGER & POULTERER.

Letterhead from an 1883 invoice featuring an illustration of 5 Swanston Street
SOURCE: STATE LIBRARY OF VICTORIA

Brougham and Dryburgh Streets. These were a house at 244 (now 486), an allotment with a stable at 246 (now 488), the vacant corner block 248 and the adjacent property east at 25 Brougham Street, which was a house with six stables at the rear.[2] Jenkins needed somewhere for his horses as there were no stables behind 'Park View'. (Langford had retained his stables at 3 Curran Place.) Jenkins decided to continue the name from his old address to the new one, renaming Milton Hall 'Park View'.[3] The new name was inscribed in gold lettering on the window above the front door.

Percy's father Joseph was well established as a fishmonger by the late 1870s. Percy's brothers Thomas and Phillip were involved in fish mongering and auctioneering at various times. In August 1881 Percy submitted a letter to Council Markets Committee successfully requesting permission to begin auctioning fish at the Swanston Street fish markets. He also opened a fish shop the same year at 5 Swanston Street next to Young and Jackson's Hotel, opposite St Paul's Cathedral. A description of this was included in the *Jubilee History of Victoria and Melbourne Illustrated,* published in 1888.

> The largest and most popular market in Melbourne for the sale of fish and game is conducted by P. N. Jenkins, in Swanston Street, near the corner of Flinders Street. This establishment commands an extensive trade, which has been built up in consequence of the proprietor keeping only the best of everything. In the sale of such perishable delica-

> cies as fish and game the utmost caution must be exercised, and, in consequence of Mr Jenkins giving his personal supervision to this department of the business, the public has long learned that they can implicitly rely on this market for all that they require. Every variety of fish and game found in the Southern Hemisphere is secured by Mr Jenkins, who spares no expense in catering to the wants of his thousands of patrons. From the morning until closing time at night the shop is thronged with citizens from all parts of the city and suburbs, securing tit bits with which to grace their tables. Mr Jenkins is without a successful rival in his line and well deserves his success.[4]

The interior of the shop was comfortably fitted out for the selling and consumption of various seafoods. The ground floor rooms were furnished with display cases, mirrors, a large and small aquarium, marble tables, pedestals and a dozen palm ferns. The oyster room contained chairs, a mirror and wooden stands. Upstairs there was a dining room, kitchen and offices. The dining room contained marble tables (with chairs), mirrors, a wall clock, dividing screens and a stag's head. There were iceboxes for storage, and Percy had an additional store nearby on Flinders Lane where he kept a bewildering array of stock.[5]

What prosperity Percy enjoyed as a businessman faded somewhat during the late 1890s. He continued trading at the fish market after its relocation to a new building at the western end of Flinders Street in 1890, taking out stand 21.[6] He took out an auctioneer's licence and began holding general sales which included dairy produce, poultry, furniture and other goods. He mortgaged 'Park View' to the Bank of Victoria in June 1891. He tendered for a lease of shops 2 and 3 in the old Swanston Street building in September 1894 for a 'fish and poultry shop', but then promptly withdrew.[7]

The family moved to 'Burwood' on St Kilda Road, Park View being rented out. Tenants included a civil servant, Joseph P. Hayes, Mrs Mary Anne Telford, and a dentist, Dr J. J. Foster, who had a surgery at 11 Swanston Street, several doors down from Percy's fish shop. Rent paid on the house was £2-10-0 per week.[8]

When Percy died of 'apoplexy' in August of that year, the extent of his deteriorating finances became fully evident. His assets were worth £12 086-7-9, with outstanding liabilities at £14 344-6-1; much of this deficit was attributable to fallen property values.[9] Resolving the estate took some time, with many outstanding business accounts requiring collection. The Equity Trustee Executors handled the resolution on behalf of Matilda.[10] Robert Langford provided some assistance, tabling a statutory declaration as part of Percy's life insurance claim, and helping prepare the sale of the businesses.

Park View was valued at £1200, with possession transferred to the Bank of Victoria. The properties at the corner of Brougham and Dryburgh Streets were valued at £1177, and were later sold to the Catholic Church, which built St Michael's Church on part of the land in 1907. Percy had also owned a block of vacant land in

Collingwood, and in Northcote, and a timber holiday cottage on land at Scoresby at Mornington. Included in the estate were 13 horses, eight sets of harnesses, six carts, a lorry, two buggies, a trap and a wagonette.[11]

The valuation of Jenkins's businesses included detailed inventories of shop furniture, fittings, and stock. The fish mongering business was sold to Henry Benjamin Hanton and 5 Swanston Street was later incorporated into Young and Jackson's Hotel in the late 1910s and remodelled.[12]

One of the Jenkins daughters, Maud, became a well-known soprano and understudy of Dame Nellie Melba, performing under the stage name Maud Harrington. She married the musician Alberto Zelman in 1912, having first met him as a member of the Musgrave Grand Opera Company in 1901. A grandson was Graham Jenkins, a war correspondent for Reuters in Indonesia, Vietnam and China, and founder of the Hong Kong Foreign Correspondents' Club.

Alterations

- The most detailed documentary evidence describing the property during this period are 1896 MMBW records (see chapters 7 and 9). It is unclear what alterations Jenkins may have made after purchasing Milton Hall from Langford.

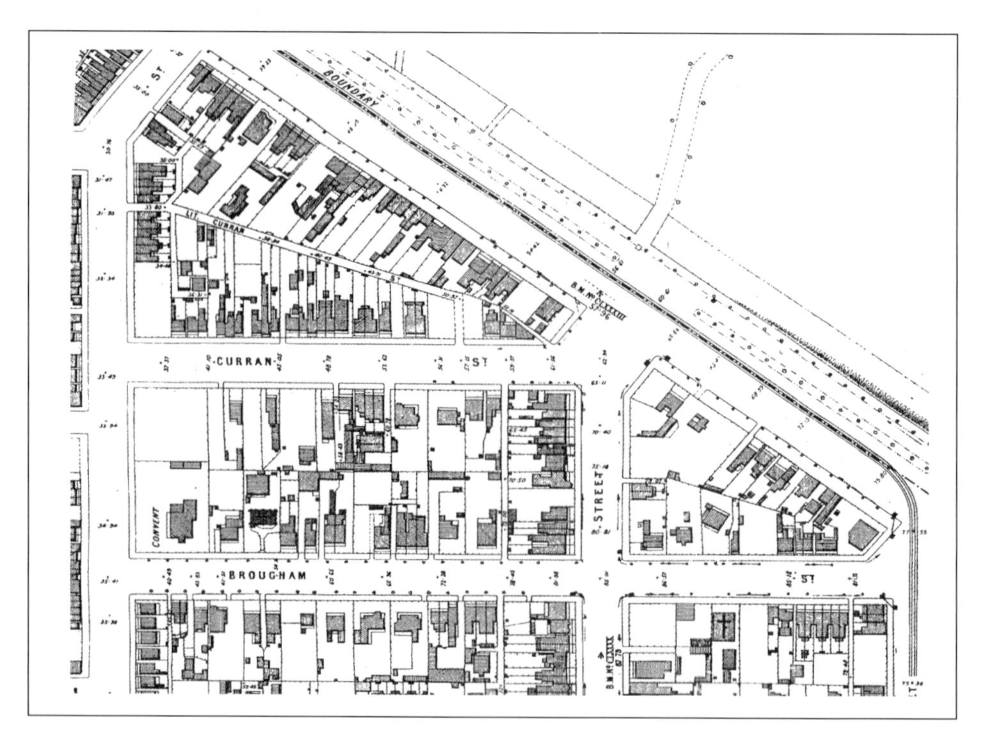

1896 MMBW Plan showing the close development of the Hotham Hill Neighbourhood by this time.
SOURCE: STATE LIBRARY OF VICTORIA.

Tenants 1901-1911

'The Vulcan Factory' at 19 Bedford Street, North Melbourne, where Pitt manufactured iron safes. SOURCE: STATE LIBRARY OF VICTORIA.

Biographical notes

Thomas Pitt leased Park View from the Bank of Victoria from 1901 to 1911. The son of a carpenter, he was born in Lepton, England, in 1829. He probably arrived in Melbourne on the *Earl of Charlemont* in June of 1853. He married Isabella McPherson at Emerald Hill eight years later, the couple eventually having 12 children. By 1901, 72-year-old Pitt was probably looking for a place to which to retire. A long career in engineering included several decades running a safe-making factory in Hotham.

In an 1888 entry in *Victoria and its Metropolis Past and Present*, the factory was thus described:

> Pitt, J., and Co, North Melbourne. This firm of manufacturers of burglar and fire-proof safes, wrought-iron pipes, &c., carry on business at the Vulcan Factory, 19 Bedford Street, North Melbourne (Hotham). Mr T. Pitt, the sole proprietor, came to Victoria in 1853, having previously learned his business at Birmingham. For the first fifteen years he was connected with engineering at various goldfields in Victoria, principally at Stawell, and at

> other places, until about 1878, when he established his present industry in a small way in Elizabeth Street, employing only himself and two boys. Business gradually increased, and he removed into his present premises in 1885, and now, on average, employs ten hands, and turns out about 120 safes each year, and about fifty to sixty strong-room doors. He was rewarded a silver medal at the Victorian Jubilee Exhibition for general excellence, that being the only time he has exhibited. His premises are large and commodious – 66 ft. wide by a depth of 166 ft. – and extremely well adapted for his business. He obtained the contract for supplying the Victorian Government with safes, first for three and then for another three years, and has supplied it with over 600 safes. The machinery, comprising drilling machines, punching presses, shearing and punching machines, &c., is driven by a 4 h.p. steam engine. A simple but very ingenious device is applied to safe and strong-room door-locks, that must recommend itself to the approval of merchants, bankers and others, by which, after unlocking the safe, the key cannot be withdrawn without locking it again. Another branch of Mr Pitt's business is the manufacture of wrought-iron hydraulic sluice pipes, in which he does a very large trade, and for which he has special machinery erected.[13]

The factory site is now occupied by the Old Melbourne Hotel. Pitt moved to Parkville in 1911, where he died in 1913, leaving an estate of £885.[14] [15]

Owners 1911-1923

Biographical notes

Edward Mylrea purchased Parkview in 1912. He was born in Ballarat in 1865, his father a miner from Liverpool and his mother a young immigrant who had gone to Ballarat 'at the height of its gold producing years' to work as a servant. Edward described himself as a warehouseman at the time of his marriage to Mary Jane Ramsey in 1892, and at other times a builder and engineer. When the couple acquired 285 Dryburgh Street in 1912, the eldest three of their four children – Mary, Lilian, Edward and Dorothy – were adults. The younger Edward studied at Melbourne University to become a veterinarian.

A regular visitor to the house would have been Edward's brother Ernest, who was Head Teacher of Rural Training School No. 307 in Errol Street.[16]

Mrs Mylrea died at age 50 in December 1921, her funeral procession moving from the family home to Williamstown cemetery. Edward sold the house in November 1923.

Alterations

- 285 Dryburgh Street renumbered 519 in 1916/17.

Edward & Mary Mylrea, with probably their first child Mary, in the 1890s. SOURCE: PHOTOGRAPH COURTESY ANDRE WRIGHT.

Owners 1923-1947

Biographical notes

Charles Henry Ringrose was born in Hobart in 1871. He married Elizabeth Kromer there in 1891 and the couple had six sons – Charles (Eric), Archibald, Douglas, Sidney, Clarence and Reginald. Charles Henry was a stevedore by occupation. The family lived in Hobart until moving to Melbourne in about 1918. They lived at 81 Capel Street in West Melbourne for a few years before purchasing 519 Dryburgh Street in 1923. Charles is thought to have paid 20 gold sovereigns for the house. By this time the children ranged in age from 11 to 29. During the late 1920s Doug Ringrose played for the Fitzroy Football Club.

The house was converted to a boarding house in 1936, probably because of a combination of tighter economic circumstances and older children moving out.[17] Typically, as the woman of the household, it was Elizabeth Ringrose who managed the rental arrangements. Rooms were usually rented out to newly married couples. Various family members lived in the house at different times, the grandparents in the ground floor front room, with others in the upstairs rear wing. (Sometimes grandchildren would sleep up in the tower.) Charles Henry died at home in 1938 aged 67.[18]

During the Second World War, Royal Park became a massive camp for Australian and American armed forces, the area south of Elliot Avenue and bordered by Flemington Road known as Camp Pell. After her husband's death, Elizabeth travelled extensively. She died tragically on 10 March 1946 along with a niece when a DC-4 in which they were passengers crashed into the sea near Hobart's Cambridge airport.[19] Her estate valued 519 Dryburgh Street at £1675, with furniture and household effects coming to £251-13-6 and goodwill on the boarding house amounting to a further £635-16-0.

The house was sold with Treasury approval to John and Lillian Ross in late 1947, at a final sale value of £2400.[20] It was resold in 1949.

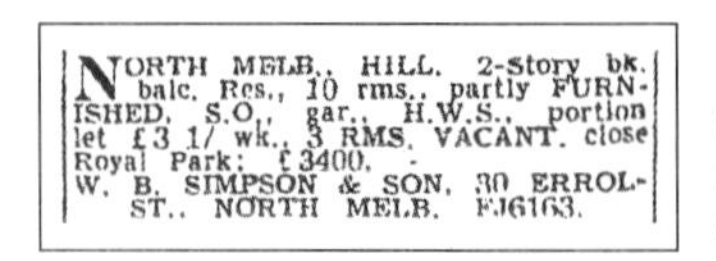

NORTH MELB., HILL. 2-Story bk. balc. Res., 10 rms., partly FURNISHED. S.O., gar., H.W.S., portion let £3 1/ wk., 3 RMS. VACANT. close Royal Park: £3400. -
W. B. SIMPSON & SON, 30 ERROL-ST., NORTH MELB. FJ6163.

Sales notice for 519 Dryburgh Street, 5 November 1949.
SOURCE: *ARGUS*

Boarding houses in the 1930s

The change in the house's occupancy from single family to multiple tenancy reflected a broader trend in the early decades of the 20th century. It has been estimated that boarding houses, lodging houses and other similar forms of communal living accounted for 5-10% of the accommodation needs of Melbourne's population between 1900 and 1950, serving all classes of society.[21] While this type of accommodation had existed since the early years of the colony, it rose markedly in popularity in the first two decades of the century. There were approximately 2364 boarding and lodging houses in Victoria in 1901, accommodating about 18 255 people (or 3.7% of the population); by 1921 this has risen to 5655 houses, accommodating about 62 205 people (or 8% of the population). The largest concentration was within the boundaries of the City of Melbourne. While the changed economic circumstances of the depression of the 1930s made this a more significant sector of the housing market, it reinforced a trend that was already widely established.[22]

Elizabeth Ringrose
SOURCE: *ARGUS*

Beginning with the passage of the *Health Act* in 1919, the operation of boarding houses became increasingly regulated by State governments. Boarding houses often provided meals for residents. The 1919 Act defined a boarding house as a place in which five occupants 'were lodged or boarded for hire or reward from week to week, or for more than one week'. [23] It allowed for the inspection of boarding houses to ensure basic standards of hygiene and cleanliness with respect to food preparation and general living conditions including sanitation. New boarding houses had to meet minimal requirements with respect to living space per tenant, food storage, natural lighting, ventilation and fire safety. Verandahs or balconies were not to be used as kitchens, and there were restrictions on their use as sleep-outs. The Act did not come into effect until 1924. Not surprisingly, it was controversial with boarding house operators, who lobbied for its revision. The new regulations passed in 1926 included mandatory provision of a common room.[24] Further tighter regulations passed in 1928 included a requirement for the keeping of a registry of tenants, and standards for cleaning regimes, and provision of linen. Local councils were involved with overseeing compliance with the new regulations.[25]

Alterations

No building permit applications were lodged with the City of Melbourne relating to the apartment conversions, thus making it difficult to precisely document associated physical changes to the house.

- Erection of new 9 feet high 26 gauge iron fence along north and west property boundaries incorporating a gate onto the north verandah and two gates onto Langford's Lane (1929). Original front fence replaced by this time.
- Timber framed fernery or glasshouse erected beneath north verandah by about this time.
- Outbuildings on site include timber garage opening onto Langford's Lane.

Owners 1949-1968

Biographical notes

Margot Pretty was born in Victoria at Woods Point 1877. Her father, Alexander Reid, was a miner and her mother's maiden name was Mary Cronan. In 1911 aged 33, Margot married Walter Pretty in Richmond. The couple had no children, though there were stepchildren from Walter's earlier marriage. Walter died in 1930.

Margot paid £4000 for the house and associated business in late 1949. She is thought to have held interests in hotels and sandwich shops in the area. At this time the front eight rooms of the house were being leased. Margot continued to run the building as a boarding house until the mid-1960s, relying on the tenant's rent for income. It was a community in miniature, with its own rituals, and patterns of private and communal space. Margot lived in the upper rear wing, serving meals to her boarders in the living room below. One of her more eccentric boarders is remembered for feeding all the local cats, while locals recall a pet cockatoo that would sit on the front fence and interact with the local children. (It was eventually stolen.) Margot died in March 1968 aged 89. The house was valued at $12 500 by this time.[26] Park View was auctioned on 26 October 1968.

W. B. Simpson & Son

Auctioneers, 30 Errol St., North Melbourne. 30 1213, RESI.

THIS DAY, At 10.30, a.m.
519 DRYBURGH STREET,
Corner Curran Street,
One Block Flemington Road and Royal Park.

North Melbourne Hill

DF BRK. BALCONY RESIDENCE
VACANT POSSESSION
Front Garden, Tiled Verandah, 11 Rooms Two Bathrooms, Kitchenette, Garage, Internal and External Toilets, HWS. LAND: 40 Ft. x 121 Ft. R. of W. at Rear.

[illegible] & O'Heare, Solicitors, 465 Collins St., Melbourne.

W. B. SIMPSON & SON.

Auction notice for 519 Dryburgh Street, 26 October 1968.
SOURCE: *ARGUS.*

C.1950s photograph showing the front entry gate in its original location, and partially enclosed balconies.
SOURCE: NORTH MELBOURNE LIBRARY

North Melbourne in the 1950s & 1960s

The post-war era saw new trends in North Melbourne's pattern of urban development, most notably flats as a building type.

Flats emerged as a more common residential typology, with single, freestanding dwellings being replaced by multi-storeyed blocks of flats. The number in North Melbourne rose from 16 in 1950 to 52 by 1969.[27] Many of these comprised small blocks of up to a dozen units replacing existing dwellings on small sites. In Curran Street, a four-storeyed block of flats was built at number 7, replacing a single occupancy, freestanding Victorian villa. An exception to this relatively low scale development was a group of three high-rise apartment blocks built on the west side of Melrose Street between Sutton and Alfred Streets during the 1960s. These became significant new local landmarks. A large proportion of North Melbourne's new flats was built by the Victorian Housing Commission.

North Melbourne also became increasingly multi-cultural from this period onwards, as European post-war migrants began settling in the area.

Alterations

- Construction of new brick WC attached to main house at a cost of £75 (1957).
- Original lookout tower disappears during this period.

HUGH O'NEILL

1968 - present

Biographical notes [28]

Hugh O'Neill's great grandparents Robert and Elizabeth (nee Murray) Aitken lived in Villiers Street, North Melbourne during the 1850s and 1860s. His maternal grandmother, Robina Wilhelmina, was born there in 1869. Four of the six surviving Aitken children subsequently lived in North Melbourne, Parkville and Park Street, Brunswick. Hugh's mother, from the next generation, married John O'Neill of the pioneering mechanical lift and public lighting company Edminston and O'Neill. They were both living in Park Street, Brunswick, and in 1929 built their new family home in Studley Park, Kew.

Hugh studied architecture at The University of Melbourne and worked in Melbourne, Indonesia and London before being appointed lecturer at the university in 1961. In 1969 he and his wife Roma and five children moved from Parkville to 519 Dryburgh Street after completing modest renovations, converting the boarding house into a family home. Sadly, Roma died in April 1979.

Park View has accommodated many visitors and sojourners. The top 'party' room is remembered as the popular meeting place for the Indonesian Arts Society of Victoria since its foundation in 1974. The building featured in a television commercial for Four 'n' Twenty Pies during the 1970s.

Hugh O'Neill and family
SOURCE: PHOTOGRAPH COURTESY HUGH O'NEILL.

Curran Street, view looking west from Dryburgh Street, 2004.

Alterations

- Most outbuildings destroyed by fire (1969).
- New timber fence erected around property perimeter at a cost of $700, with single entry gate from Dryburgh Street (1969).
- Original tiled entry path to front door from Dryburgh Street eliminated (1969).
- Purple Bougainvillea vine planted (1969).
- Various internal alterations undertaken, at a cost of $4000. House converted back into a single residence. Partitions of c.1936 and rear servants' stair removed. Pitched roof constructed over the tower platform. A modern kitchen and modern bathrooms installed. Former pantry/coolroom converted into a bathroom (1969).

Appendix A

Langford family tree

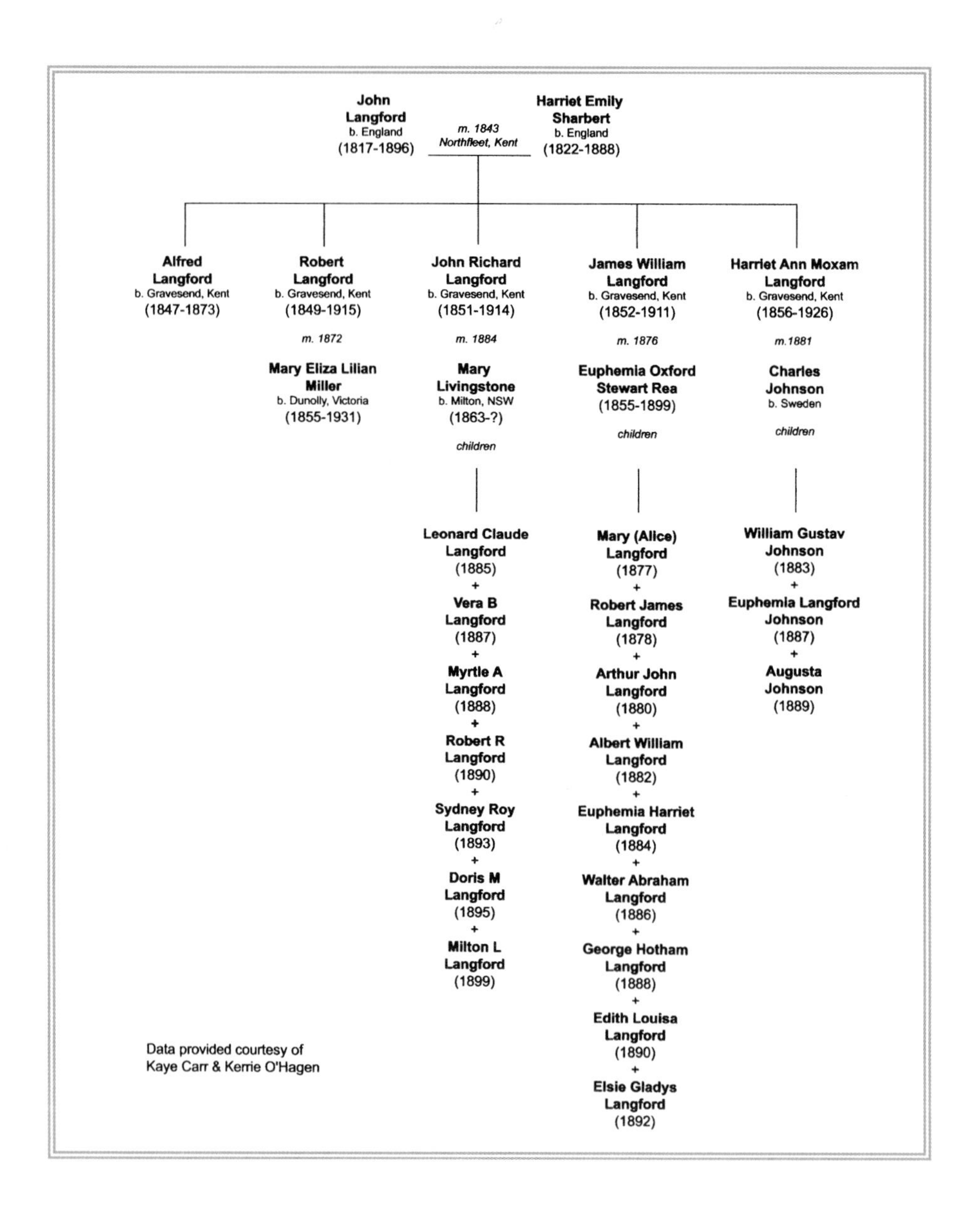

Appendix B

Real estate holdings of Robert Langford in two years prior to June 1895

(Compiled from PROV VPRS 763/P, Unit 22, File C239 and original land titles.)

No	Location	Title number	Area	Value	Acquisition date	Date of any mortgages, & whom to	Date of sale/transferral
1	Crown Allotment 18, Section 6, Parish of Boroondara, County of Bourke.	Volume 1417, Folio 283270	1 rood, 26 8/10 perches	£2000	25/04/1887	17/10/1892 Commercial Bank of Australia Ltd	1/5/1905 Transferred to bank
2	Part of Crown Portion 26, Parish of Nunawading, County of Bourke	Volume 1456, Folio 291027	3 acres, 2 roods, 4 5/10 perches	£400	12/04/1883	17/10/1892 Commercial Bank of Australia Ltd	29/12/1916 Transferred to bank
3	Crown Allotment 246B, Parish of Bairnsdale, County of Tanjil	Volume 1601, Folio 320192	100 acres, 3 roods, 8 perches	£250	28/11/1888	17/10/1892 Commercial Bank of Australia Ltd	19/10/1909 Transferred to bank
4	Lot 36 in Subdivision 1572, part of Crown Allotment 147A and 147B in the Parish of Bairnsdale, County of Tanjil	Volume 1941, Folio 388102	-	£10	16/08/1888	17/10/1892 Commercial Bank of Australia Ltd	27/01/1915 Transferred to bank
5	Lots 17 and 18 in Subdivision 1468, part of Crown Portion 9, Parish of Nunawading, County of Bourke	Volume 1992, Folio 398374	-	£50	12/02/1888	17/10/1892 Commercial Bank of Australia Ltd	Date unknown
6	Crown Allotments 1 and 2, Section 7, Parish of Sale, County of Tanjil	Volume 1101, Folio 220015	8 acres, 3 roods, 3 perches	£400	17/10/1892	04/09/1879 To Robert Richardson, paid. 17/10/1892 Commercial Bank of Australia Ltd	11/05/1896 Transferred to bank
7	Part of Crown Allotment 18, Section 6, Parish of Boroondara, County of Bourke	Volume 1229, Folio 245695	1 rood, 7 1/10 perches	£520	25/04/1887	17/10/1892	01/05/1905 Transferred to bank
8	Crown Allotment 246C, Parish of Bairnsdale, County of Tanjil	Volume 2116, Folio 423184	46 acres, 32 perches	£115	13/12/1888	17/10/1892 Commercial Bank of Australia Ltd	19/10/1909 Transferred to bank
9	Part of Section A, Parish of Bairnsdale, County of Tanjil	Volume 2171, Folio 434134	-	£100	08/07/1889	17/10/1892 Commercial Bank of Australia Ltd	Date unknown Transferred to bank
10	Lots 54 to 74 and 84 and 85 in Subdivision 1760, parts of Elgar Crown Special Survey, Parish of Boroondara, County of Bourke	Volume 2184, Folio 436605	4 acres, 1 rood, 5 6/10 perches	£575	12/08/1889	17/10/1892 Commercial Bank of Australia Ltd	Date unknown Transferred to bank

No	Location	Title number	Area	Value	Acquisition date	Date of any mortgages, & whom to	Date of sale/transferral
7	Part of Crown Allotment 18, Section 6, Parish of Boroondara, County of Bourke	Volume 1229, Folio 245695	1 rood, 7 1/10 perches	£520	25/04/1887	17/10/1892	01/05/1905 Transferred to bank
8	Crown Allotment 246C, Parish of Bairnsdale, County of Tanjil	Volume 2116, Folio 423184	46 acres, 32 perches	£115	13/12/1888	17/10/1892 Commercial Bank of Australia Ltd	19/10/1909 Transferred to bank
9	Part of Section A, Parish of Bairnsdale, County of Tanjil	Volume 2171, Folio 434134	-	£100	08/07/1889	17/10/1892 Commercial Bank of Australia Ltd	Date unknown Transferred to bank
10	Lots 54 to 74 and 84 and 85 in Subdivision 1760, parts of Elgar Crown Special Survey, Parish of Boroondara, County of Bourke	Volume 2184, Folio 436605	4 acres, 1 rood, 5 6/10 perches	£575	12/08/1889	17/10/1892 Commercial Bank of Australia Ltd	Date unknown Transferred to bank
16	Crown Allotment 13, Section 1B, Township of Carisbrook, Parish of Carisbrook, County of Talbot	Volume 429, Folio 85641	26 perches	£5	16/05/1890	16/05/1890 William Webb & Jean/John Baptiste Loridan, paid.	08/11/1895
17	Crown Allotment 1, Section 54, Parish of Carisbrook, County of Talbot	Volume 595, Folio 118982	1 acre, 30 perches	£7	16/05/1890	16/05/1890 William Webb & Jean/John Baptiste Loridan, paid.	14/01/1898
18	Crown Allotment 2, Section 54, Parish of Carisbrook, County of Talbot	Volume 595, Folio 118983	1 acre, 39 perches	£10	16/05/1890	16/05/1890 William Webb & Jean/John Baptiste Loridan, paid.	14/01/1898
19	Crown Allotment 3, Section 54, Parish of Carisbrook, County of Talbot	Volume 595, Folio 118984	1 acre, 1 rood, 20 perches	£7	16/05/1890	16/05/1890 William Webb & Jean/John Baptiste Loridan, paid.	14/01/1898
20	Crown Allotment 4, Section 54, Parish of Carisbrook, County of Talbot	Volume 595, Folio 118985	1 acre, 2 roods, 6 perches	£10	16/05/1890	16/05/1890 William Webb & Jean/John Baptiste Loridan, paid.	14/01/1898
21	Crown Allotment 5, Section 54, Parish of Carisbrook, County of Talbot	Volume 595, Folio 118986	1 acre, 2 roods	£8	16/05/1890	16/05/1890 William Webb & Jean/John Baptiste Loridan, paid.	14/01/1898
22	Crown Allotment 6, Section 54, Parish of Carisbrook, County of Talbot	Volume 595, Folio 118987	1 acre, 2 perches	£7	16/05/1890	16/05/1890 William Webb & Jean/John Baptiste Loridan, paid.	14/01/1898
23	Crown Allotment 7, Section 54, Parish of Carisbrook, County of Talbot	Volume 595, Folio 118988	1 acre, 1 rood, 10 perches	£10	16/05/1890	16/05/1890 William Webb & Jean/John Baptiste Loridan, paid.	14/01/1898
24	Crown Allotment 8, Section 54, Parish of Carisbrook, County of Talbot	Volume 595, Folio 118989	1 acre, 2 roods	£8	16/05/1890	16/05/1890 William Webb & Jean/John Baptiste Loridan, paid.	14/01/1898
25	Crown Allotment 9, Section 54, Parish of Carisbrook, County of Talbot	Volume 595, Folio 118990	1 acre, 2 roods	£8	16/05/1890	16/05/1890 William Webb & Jean/John Baptiste Loridan, paid.	14/01/1898
26	Crown Allotment 10, Section 54, Parish of Carisbrook, County of Talbot	Volume 595, Folio 118991	1 acre, 1 rood, 12 perches	£7	16/05/1890	16/05/1890 William Webb & Jean/John Baptiste Loridan, paid.	14/01/1898
27	Crown Allotment 11, Section 54, Parish of Carisbrook, County of Talbot	Volume 595, Folio 118992	1 acre	£10	16/05/1890	16/05/1890 William Webb & Jean/John Baptiste Loridan, paid.	14/01/1898

28	Crown Allotment 12, Section 54, Parish of Carisbrook, County of Talbot	Volume 595, Folio 118993	3 roods, 32 perches	£7	16/05/1890	16/05/1890 William Webb & Jean/John Baptiste Loridan, paid.	14/01/1898
29	Crown Allotment 13, Section 54, Parish of Carisbrook, County of Talbot	Volume 595, Folio 118994	1 acre, 1 rood	£7	16/05/1890	16/05/1890 William Webb & Jean/John Baptiste Loridan, paid.	14/01/1898
30	Crown Allotment 14, Section 54, Parish of Carisbrook, County of Talbot	Volume 595, Folio 118995	1 acre, 39 perches	£7	16/05/1890	16/05/1890 William Webb & Jean/John Baptiste Loridan, paid.	14/01/1898
31	Crown Allotment 1, Section 1C, Parish and Town of Carisbrook, County of Talbot	Volume 635, Folio 126951	2 roods, 25 1/2 perches	£7	16/05/1890	16/05/1890 William Webb & Jean/John Baptiste Loridan, paid.	08/11/1895
32	Lots 31 and 58 in Subdivision 1951, part of portion 12, Parish of Mulgrave, County of Bourke	Volume 2133, Folio 426499	-	£5	18/02/1891	Impounded through court order.	06/02/1911
33	Lot 62 in Subdivision 1128, part of Section A known as Dendy's Pre-emptive Right, Parish of Frankston, County of Mornington	Volume 2302, Folio 460397	5 acres, 2 roods, 16 perches	£30	08/10/1890	None	06/02/1911
34	Crown Allotments 1 -10, Section 22, Township of Carisbrook, Parish of Carisbrook, County of Talbot	Volume 2173, Folio 434480	6 acres, 3 roods, 4 8/10 perches	£400	16/05/1890	16/05/1890 William Webb & Jean/John Baptiste Loridan, paid.	13/10/1895
35	Land with a frontage of 24 feet to Munro Street, Ascot Vale, by a depth of 150 feet	-	-	£100	-	-	-
36	Land with a frontage of 26 feet to George Street, North Melbourne, by a depth of 84 feet	-	-	£100	-	-	-
37	Lot 44 in Subdivision 1572, part of Crown Allotment 147B in the Parish of Bairnsdale, County of Tanjil	Volume 1962, Folio 392350	-	£5	11/12/1891	Not identified	- Not identified

Re: 32
Copy decree issued out of the county court in plaint [sic] No 1190 in the year 1910, the President, Councillors and Ratepayers of the Shire of Mulgrave against Robert Langford, Rachel Cooper and Harry Kosken [sic] served on 25th January, 1911. Transfer of title occurred 6 February, 1911.

The title for (2) relates to land bordered by Barkley Road, Canterbury Road and Bedford Street around its east, west and south sides.

Notes

Chapter One

[1] William Page (editor), *A History of Kent* (Volume 3), p. 362.
[2] Elizabeth Brabazon, *A Month at Gravesend*, p. 9.
[3] A. J. Philip, *A History of Gravesend*, 1914, Volume 1.
[4] The following description draws heavily from James Benson, *A History of Gravesend*, 1976.
[5] Kent Town Council, *Gravesend and Neighbourhood*, p. 20.
[6] Benson, op. cit.
[7] Brabazon, op. cit. p. 43.
[8] Barrie Dyster, & David Meredeth, *Australia in the International Economy*, p. 21.
[9] Geoffrey Blainey, *The Tyranny of Distance*, p. 184.
[10] Ibid, p. 193.
[11] Character reference for John Langford from inhabitants of Gravesend 1857, from 'Grandfather Langford's Testimonial', manuscript held by Langford family.
[12] *Argus*, 9 February 1858, p. 4.
[13] *Argus*, 9 February 1858.
[14] *Argus*, 27 March 1858, p. 1.
[15] Phillip Rayson, Correspondence 1858-1860, MS 3895-97, Box 28/5, Royal Historical Society of Victoria.
[16] Blainey, op cit, p. 159-60.
[17] Blainey, loc. cit.
[18] Rayson, op. cit.
[19] Blainey, loc. cit.
[20] Rayson, loc. cit.
[21] Rayson, loc. cit.
[22] Geoffrey Blainey, op. cit., pp. 179-80.
[23] Rayson, loc. cit.
[24] *Argus*, 9 February 1858.
[25] *Argus*, 1 April 1858, p. 4.
[26] Olaf Ruhen, *Port of Melbourne 1835-1876*, p. 104.
[27] *Argus*, 9 February 1858.

Chapter Two

[1] Asa Briggs, Victorian Cities, Chapter 7 "Melbourne, a Victorian Community Overseas".
[2] Briggs, op. cit. p. 283.
[3] Michael Cannon, *Melbourne After the Gold Rush*, p. 371.
[4] Colin E. Cole (editor), *Melbourne's Markets 1841-1979*, pp. 34-6.
[5] Cannon, op. cit., p. 187.
[6] Character reference for John Langford from inhabitants of Gravesend 1857, from 'Grandfather Langford's Testimonial', manuscript held by Langford family.
[7] Cole (editor), op. cit., p. 93.
[8] Cole (editor), ibid, p. 3.
[9] H. H. Paynting & Malcolm Grant, *Victoria Illustrated 1834-1984*, 1984, p. 134.
[10] Cole (editor), op. cit., p. 91.
[11] Cannon, op. cit., p. 187.
[12] *Melbourne Leader*, 31 July 1858, p. 11.
[13] Kathleen Thomson and Geoffrey Serle, *A Biographical Register of the Victorian Parliament 1851-1900*, 163.
[14] Advertisements for his company in the 1890s list an establishment date for the business of 1866. See *Romsey Examiner*, 7 May 1897.

[15] PROV, VPRS 4030/P/4.
[16] John Freeman, *Lights and Shadows of Melbourne Life,* p. 163.
[17] Freeman, ibid, p. 158.
[18] Graeme Davison (ed.), *The Outcasts of Melbourne*, p. 16.
[19] *Romsey Examiner*, Friday 4 June 1897.
[20] Michael Clarke, *Clarke of Rupertswood 1831-1897*, pp. 43, 60-3.
[21] Testimonial of Louise Macdonald (Miller), manuscript held by the Maryborough Library.
[22] The first theatre had opened illegally in 1841. While a Mr W. Miller was listed as a stage manager and performer for its opening night, whether this was Elizabeth Miller's father is uncertain. Katherine Brisbane (editor), *Entertaining Australia*, p. 36.
[23] Alec Bagot, *Coppin the Great*, pp. 41-42.
[24] Bagot, loc. cit.
[25] What happened to his first wife and their four children is unclear.
[26] W. J. Lawrence, *The Life of Gustavus Vaughan Brooke*, p. 262. Note: Miller is not mentioned in the several biographies of Brooke.
[27] James Flett, *Dunolly,* p. 114.
[28] Seweryn Korzelinski, *Memoirs of Gold Digging in Australia*, p. 38.
[29] Flett, op. cit., p. 41.
[30] Testimonial of Louise Macdonald (Miller), manuscript held by the Maryborough Library.
[31] Testimonial of Louise Macdonald (Miller).
[32] Jules Verne, *On the Track*, p. 83.
[33] Testimonial of Louise Macdonald (Miller).
[34] PROV, VPRS 7591/P/2, Unit 222, File 54/782.
[35] Testimonial of Louise Macdonald (Miller), manuscript held by the Maryborough Library.
[36] Ibid.

Chapter 3

[1] PROV, VPRS 4030/P/3, p. 675.
[2] Bruce Bennett, *The Fishmarkets of Melbourne*, p. I.
[3] *Sands & McDougall Directory* and Bennett, op. cit., pp. 5, 26, 28, 29, 53.
[4] Proceedings of Inquest of Alfred John Langford, PROV, VPRS 7591/P2, Unit 503, File 132/452.
[5] PROV, VPRS 4030/P/4, pp. 177-8.
[6] PROV, VPRS 4030/P/4, p. 101.
[7] PROV, VPRS 4030/P/4, p. 222.
[8] PROV, VPRS 4030/P/4, p. 228.
[9] PROV, VPRS 4030/P/4, pp. 424-5, 431.
[10] PROV, VPRS 4030/P/4, p. 432.
[11] PROV, VPRS 4030/P/4, p. 440.
[12] PROV, VPRS 4030/P/5, pp. 16-17.
[13] PROV, VPRS 4030/P/4, p. 301.
[14] PROV, VPRS 4030/P/4, pp. 439-40.
[15] *North Melbourne Advertiser*, 30 November 1883.
[16] *Sands & McDougall Directory* and Bennett, op. cit, pp. 26, 29, 32.
[17] Bennett, op. cit., p. 35.
[18] Testimonial of Louise Macdonald (Miller).
[19] *North Melbourne Advertiser,* 19 March 1886.
[20] Bennett, op. cit., p.115.
[21] *Sands and McDougall Directory,* 1885.

Chapter 4

[1] Norman Tingle, *Aboriginal Tribes of Australia,* pp. 208-9.
[2] Jared Diamond, *Guns, Germs and Steel*, pp. 44-5.
[3] Alastair Campbell, *John Batman and the Aborigines*, p. 74.
[4] Michael Cannon, *Old Melbourne Town Before the Gold Rushes*, p. 175.
[5] Miles Lewis, *Melbourne: The City's History and Development*, p. 18.
[6] Cannon, op. cit., p. 174.
[7] Michael Cannon, *Melbourne After the Gold Rush*, p. 267-9.
[8] Ibid.
[9] From Certificate of Title of 519 Dryburgh Street, Volume 1130, Folio 225882, Lands Victoria.
[10] It appears on an 1861 Crown Lands Office Map of Melbourne and its Suburbs, the northern end of Dryburgh Street having also been laid out by this time. See Crown Lands Office Map of Melbourne and its Suburbs, (copy held at Maps Library, Education Resource Centre, University of Melbourne).
[11] Edmund Finn ('Garryowen'), *The Chronicles of Early Melbourne*, p. 30.
[12] *The New Encyclopedia Britannica*, Volume 3, p. 801.
[13] *Argus*, 5 September 1865, p. 2.
[14] *Argus*, 26 August 1867, p. 2.
[15] *Argus*, 14 October 1867, p. 2.
[16] North Melbourne Rate Books.
[17] North Melbourne Rate Books.

[18] Finn, op. cit., p. 30.

[19] *Sands & McDougall Directories* 1880-1974.

[20] Hilary Lewis, *Parkville*, p. 1.

[21] Georgina Whitehead, *Royal Park Cultural Heritage Study Draft*, p. 7.

[22] John Allan (editor), *The Victorian Centenary Book*, p. 15.

[23] Michael Cannon, *Old Melbourne Town Before the Gold Rushes*, p. 175.

[24] Whitehead, op. cit., p. 8.

[25] North Melbourne Rate Books.

Chapter 5

[1] *Victorian Municipal Directory and Gazette,* 1883, pp. 38-9.

[2] *Victorian Year Book, 1893,* p. 13.

[3] *Victorian Municipal Directory and Gazette,* 1883, pp. 16-17.

[4] *North Melbourne Advertiser*, 15 July 1882.

[5] *North Melbourne Advertiser*, 10 May 1882.

[6] *North Melbourne Advertiser*, 26 May 1882.

[7] *North Melbourne Advertiser*, 2 June 1882.

[8] *North Melbourne Advertiser*, 16 June 1882.

[9] *North Melbourne Advertiser*, 14 July 1882.

[10] *North Melbourne Advertiser*, 28 July 1882.

[11] *Maryborough and Dunolly North Melbourne Advertiser*, 9 August 1882, p. 2.

[12] *North Melbourne Advertiser*, 11 August 1882.

[13] *Maryborough and Dunolly North Melbourne Advertiser*, 11 August 1882, p. 3.

[14] *Argus*, 27 August 1880.

[15] *Argus*, 27 August 1880.

[16] *North Melbourne Advertiser*, 1 September 1882.

[17] *North Melbourne Advertiser*, 22 August 1884.

[18] *Maryborough and Dunolly Advertiser*, 6 September 1882, p. 4.

[19] *North Melbourne Advertiser*, 27 October 1882.

[20] *North Melbourne Advertiser*, 23 June 1882.

[21] *North Melbourne Advertiser*, 15 September 1882.

[22] Miles Lewis, *Melbourne: The City's History and Development,* p. 68.

[23] *North Melbourne Advertiser*, 2 June 1882.

[24] *North Melbourne Advertiser*, 13 October 1882.

[25] *North Melbourne Advertiser*, 9 June 1882.

[26] *North Melbourne Advertiser*, 23 January 1883.

[27] *North Melbourne Advertiser*, 29 August 1884.

[28] *North Melbourne Advertiser*, 24 April 1885.

[29] *North Melbourne Advertiser*, 10 April 1884.

[30] *North Melbourne Advertiser*, 8 August 1884.

[31] *North Melbourne Advertiser,* 22 August 1884.

[32] *North Melbourne Advertiser*, 16 May 1884.

Chapter 6

[1] *North Melbourne Advertiser,* 16 May 1884.

[2] Mary Turner Shaw, *Builders of Melbourne,* p. 12.

[3] *Victoria and Metropolis,* Volume IIB, p. 521.

[4] Allom Lovell and Associates, *Fitzroy Town Hall Conservation Management Plan,* p. 13.

[5] *Argus*, 20 May 1871, p. 2, and *Argus,* 31 May 1875, p. 2.

[6] Dr Miles Lewis, pers. comm.

[7] There are no entries in the Australian Architectural Index relating to Langford's 1884 house, by location or under identified possible architects.

[8] Death Certificate 12944, Registry of Births, Deaths and Marriages, Victoria.

[9] *Argus*, 20 November 1884, p. 3.

[10] *Argus*, 30 January 1885, p. 3 and *Argus*, 2 May 1885, p. 14.

[11] James Smith (editor), *Cyclopedia of Victoria,* Volume 1, p. 599.

[12] Oscar Gimsey, *Built From Nothing*, pp. 57-9.

[13] It was moved in a council meeting on 7 April 1884 that the tender of Mr M. Barrett for construction of Langford's lane, section 88, for the sum of £119 16s 8d be accepted, *North Melbourne Advertiser,* 10 April 1884.

[14] North Melbourne Rate Books

Chapter 7

[1] *North Melbourne Advertiser,* 27 March 1885.

[2] *North Melbourne Advertiser,* 5 September 1884.

[3] Henry Cowan, *From Wattle and Daub to Concrete and Steel,* p. 62.

[4] E Graham Robertson, *Ornamental Cast Iron Lace in Melbourne*, p. 1.

[5] Op.cit., pp. 50, 55.

[6] Miles Lewis, 'Following the Red Brick Road'.

[7] Miles Lewis, *Physical Investigation of a Building*, p. 36.

[8] Miles Lewis, op.cit., p. 30.

[9] Terence Lockett, *Collecting Victorian Tiles,* p. 62.

[10] *North Melbourne Advertiser,* 11 June 1882.

Chapter 8

[1] *North Melbourne Advertiser*, 22 August 1884.
[2] *North Melbourne Advertiser*, 14 July 1882.
[3] *Argus*, 27 August 1880, p. 5.
[4] *North Melbourne Advertiser*, 5 September 1884.
[5] *North Melbourne Advertiser*, 5 September 1884.
[6] *North Melbourne Advertiser*, 3 October 1884.
[7] *North Melbourne Advertiser*, 31 July 1885.
[8] *North Melbourne Advertiser*, 10 April 1885.
[9] *Table Talk*, 31 July 1885.
[10] *North Melbourne Advertiser*, 7 November 1884, 13 April 1889.
[11] *North Melbourne Advertiser*, 27 March 1885.
[12] *North Melbourne Advertiser,* 14 August 1885.
[13] Bennett, op. cit., pp. 34-35.
[14] PROV, VPRS 4030/P/5, pp. 176-182.
[15] PROV, VPRS 4030/P/5, p. 152.
[16] Bennett, op. cit., pp. 34-35
[17] *North Melbourne Advertiser,* 19 March 1886.
[18] *North Melbourne Advertiser,* 11 June 1882.
[19] Gerard Dowling, *The North Story*, p. 31.
[20] *North Melbourne Advertiser*, 27 March 1885.
[21] *North Melbourne Advertiser*, 27 March 1885.
[22] *North Melbourne Advertiser*, 24 July 1885.
[23] *North Melbourne Advertiser*, 2 April 1885.
[24] Elaine Warne, *Errol Street: The First Hundred Years 1857-1957*, pp. 33-34.
[25] *North Melbourne Advertiser,* 22 May 1885.
[26] *North Melbourne Advertiser,* 10 July 1885.
[27] *North Melbourne Advertiser,* 10 July 1885.
[28] *North Melbourne Advertiser*, 23 January 1885.
[29] Robert Sands, *North Melbourne Town Hall Complex Heritage Assessment and Conservation Plan*, p. 23.
[30] Finn, op. cit., p. 29.
[31] *North Melbourne Advertiser*, 7 August 1885.
[32] *North Melbourne Advertiser*, 14 August 1885.
[33] *North Melbourne Advertiser*, 7 and 14 August 1885.
[34] *Maryborough and Dunolly Advertiser*, 12 August 1885, p. 2.

Chapter 9

[1] The sources for the names are: Milton Hall – earliest reference in the *North Melbourne Advertiser*, 5 September 1884; Gravesend – MMBW field survey sketchbook (PROV, VPRS 8600/P1, Unit 24, book 426, pp. 57-8); also death notice for Euphemia Langford, *Age*, 15 May 1899; Milton Cottage – death certificate of John Langford, 19 June 1896; Kent Cottages – see inscription on parapet.
[2] Collated from North Melbourne Rate Books and *Sands & McDougall Directories*.
[3] North Melbourne Rate Books.
[4] *Argus,* 30 January 1885 and 2 May 1885.
[5] North Melbourne Rate Books.
[6] Ibid.
[7] *Argus*, 20 November 1884.
[8] North Melbourne Rate Books.
[9] Ibid.
[10] *North Melbourne Advertiser,* 9 March 1889.
[11] Subdivision Plans LP 34460, 28522, Parish of Jika Jika, Land Victoria.
[12] North Melbourne Rate Books.
[13] *Argus,* 13 June 1885.

Chapter 10

[1] *North Melbourne Advertiser,* 9 October 1885.
[2] *North Melbourne Advertiser,* 7 October 1885.
[3] The following tender notice appeared in the *Argus,* 21 October 1885, p. 9, 'Tenders wanted for new Bible Christian Church (brick), Brougham Street, Hotham'. The building survives at 17 Brougham Street and was converted into accommodation for the elderly in 1997.
[4] *North Melbourne Advertiser*, 26 February 1886.
[5] *North Melbourne Advertiser,* 26 February 1886.
[6] *North Melbourne Advertiser,* 19 March 1886.
[7] From Certificate of Title of 519 Dryburgh Street, Volume 1130, Folio 225882, Lands Victoria.
[8] Michael Cannon, *The Land Boomers,* p.13.
[9] Certificate of Title, Volume 1837, Folio 289.
[10] John Wells, *Gippsland: People, a Place and their Past*, pp. 169-71, 256.
[11] Certificate of Title, Volume 1837, Folio 289.
[12] PROV, VPRS 763/P, Unit 22, File C239.
[13] *North Melbourne Advertiser,* 19 March 1886.
[14] *North Melbourne Advertiser,* 9 July 1887.
[15] *Maryborough and Dunolly Advertiser*, 8 June 1887, p. 4.
[16] Macedon Ranges Cultural Heritage and Landscape Study, Volume 4, pp. 619-21.
[17] See *Romsey Examiner*, 14 August 1896.
[18] *Victoria Police Gazette*, 2 April 1890, p. 111.

[19] *Victoria Police Gazette*, 28 May 1890, p. 170.

[20] George H Langford, 'Copy of My Grandfather's Testimonial', typescript held by Langford family.

[21] Margaret Corris in *Australian Dictionary of Biography*, Volume 5, 1851-1890, p.69.

[22] *North Melbourne Advertiser*, 9 March 1889.

[23] Ibid.

[24] *North Melbourne Advertiser*, 30 March 1889.

[25] *North Melbourne Advertiser*, 14 February 1890.

[26] *North Melbourne Advertiser*, 21 February 1890.

[27] *Victorian Municipal Directory and Gazette 1890*, p. 402.

[28] This building was in turn demolished in 1959, with the fish market moving to new facilities in Footscray.

Chapter 11

[1] Barrie Dyster & David Meredeth, *Australia in the International Economy*, pp. 40-4.

[2] Cannon, *The Land Boomers*, p. 19.

[3] Dyster & Meredeth, op. cit., p. 40.

[4] PROV, VPRS 4084/P/0000, Unit 2, Volume 2.

[5] PROV, VPRS 4030/P/7, p. 105.

[6] PROV, VPRS 4030/P/7, p 172.

[7] PROV, VPRS 4084/P/0000, Unit 2, Volume 2.

[8] The estate was bequeathed to William's two youngest children, Frederick John Miller and Euphemia Anne Miller. PROV, VPRS 7591/P/2, Unit 222, File 54/782.

[9] Trevor Budge & Associates, *Macedon Ranges Cultural Heritage and Landscape Study*, Volume 4, pp. 619-21.

[10] *Argus*, 11 November 1896, p. 2.

[11] *War Cry*, 26 May 1900.

[12] *Romsey Examiner*, 22 February 1885 and *Gisborne Gazette*, 10 April 1886.

[13] *Gisborne Gazette*, 25 October 1885.

[14] Ian Boyd, Gisborne Historical Society, pers. comm.

[15] *Romsey Examiner*, 5 October 1885.

[16] *Romsey Examiner*, 18 January 1886 and *Gisborne Gazette*, 11 January 1895.

[17] *Gisborne Gazette*, 1 November 1895.

[18] PROV, VPRS 763/P, Unit 22, File C239.

[19] PROV, VPRS 763/P, Unit 22, File C239.

[20] PROV, VPRS 763/P, Unit 22, File C239.

[21] PROV, VPRS 763/P, Unit 22, File C239.

[22] Cannon, *The Land Boomers*, p. 205.

[23] Compiled from PROV, VPRS 763/P, Unit 22, File C239 and original land titles.

[24] *West Bourke Times*, 28 August 1902.

[25] *Gisborne Gazette*, 2 August 1885.

[26] *Gisborne Gazette*, 28 June 1885 and *Romsey Examiner*, 4 October 1885.

[27] *Romsey Examiner*, 11 October 1895.

[28] *Romsey Examiner*, 11 December 1896.

[29] *Romsey Examiner*, 14 August 1896.

[30] *Romsey Examiner*, 29 January 1897.

[31] John Amess's diaries for 1890-93, 1899-1900 are held at the State Library (MS 12806). These record mainly farm management related events, but also references to social activities. No references are made to the Langfords.

[32] *Romsey Examiner*, 21 August 1886.

[33] *Romsey Examiner*, 28 August and 11 September 1886.

[34] *Romsey Examiner*, 23 October 1896.

[35] *Gisborne Gazette*, 6 November 1886.

[36] *Argus*, 11 November 1896, p. 2 and *Gisborne Gazette*, 13 November 1886.

[37] Trevor Budge & Associates, op. cit., pp. 619-21.

[38] *Gisborne Gazette*, 20, 27 November 1886.

[39] *Romsey Examiner*, 5 March 1897.

[40] *Romsey Examiner*, 4 June 1897 and Morissey, Sylvia, in *Australian Dictionary of Biography*, Volume 3, pp. 422-4.

[41] *Romsey Examiner*, 15 May 1897.

[42] *Romsey Examiner*, 25 June 1897.

[43] *Romsey Examiner*, 3 September 1897.

[44] Testimonial of Louise Macdonald (Miller), typescript held by the Maryborough Library.

[45] PROV, VPRS 4030/P/7, p. 177, and PROV, VPRS 4030/P/8, p. 8.

[46] PROV, VPRS 4030/P/8, p. 42.

[47] Frank Crowley (editor), *A New History of Australia*, pp. 247-67.

[48] *West Bourke Times*, 28 August 1902.

[49] *West Bourke Times*, 17 August 1905.

[50] *Flemington Spectator*, 9 October 1902.

[51] PROV, VPRS 4030/P/8, p. 414, and PROV, VPRS 4030/P/9.

[52] *Western Australian Postal Directory*, 1906-15.

[53] PROV, VPRS 28/P3, Unit 205, File 119/885.

[54] George R Langford, 'Copy of My Grandfather's Testimonial', p. 3. (Typescript held by Langford family).

[55] There is no listing of a Robert Langford in the

Victorian, New South Wales or Western Australian probate indexes.

[56] *Newtown Rate Books*

[57] The institution survives today as the Kingston Centre.

Chapter 12

[1] Compiled from North Melbourne Rate Books, *Sands & McDougall Directories* and title documents (various).

[2] North Melbourne Rate Books.

[3] A scrap book dated c.1895 which belonged to Edith Jenkins and is held by descendant Robert Cannon is inscribed with the address 'Park View'. This was also inscribed in gold lettering on the doorlight about the front door, which survived until the c.1970s, Hugh O'Neill, pers comm.

[4] T. W. H. Leavitt, (editor),*The Jubilee History of Victoria and Melbourne Illustrated*, Volume 1.

[5] PROV, VPRS 28/P/2, Unit 560, File 76/831.

[6] Bruce Bennett, *Fish Markets of Melbourne*, p. 30.

[7] PROV, VPRS 4030/P/7, p. 126.

[8] PROV, VPRS 28/P/2, Unit 560, File 76/831.

[9] Ibid.

[10] Ibid.

[11] Ibid.

[12] Bennett, op. cit., p. 30.

[13] *Victoria and its Metropolis Past and Present*, Melbourne, 1888, Volume IIB, p. 617.

[14] His death notice appeared in the *Argus* and *Age* on 10 December 1913.

[15] PROV, VPRS 28/P/3, Unit 418, 132/459.

[16] Fairlie Taylor, *Bid Time Return*, p. 128.

[17] *Sands & McDougall Directories* list apartments at this address from 1936.

[18] Adrian Ringrose, pers. comm.

[19] Macarthur Job, *Air Crash*, Volume 2, p. 40-49.

[20] PROV, VPRS 28/P/3, Unit 4303, File 375/551.

[21] Seamus O'Hanlon, *Together Apart*, 2002, p. 18.

[22] O'Hanlon, op. cit., pp. 18-25.

[23] O'Hanlon, op. cit., p. 68.

[24] O'Hanlon, op. cit., pp. 66-72.

[25] O'Hanlon, op. cit., pp. 73-76.

[26] PROV, VPRS 28/P/5, Unit 71, File 672/157.

[27] Ken Johnson, *People and Property in North Melbourne*, p.18.

[28] By Hugh O'Neill

Bibliography

Primary sources

Newspapers and journals

Age

Argus

Australasian

Flemington Spectator

Gisborne Gazette

Maryborough and Dunolly Advertiser

Melbourne Bulletin

Melbourne Leader

North Melbourne Advertiser

Romsey Examiner

Table Talk

Victoria Police Gazette

War Cry

West Bourke Times

Other published material

Hall's Gravesend & Northfleet Directory & North Melbourne Advertiser, 1840-1950.

Kelly's Directory of Kent, 1850-1900.

Sands & McDougall Melbourne Directory, 1862-1970.

Victorian Government Gazette, Government Printer, Melbourne, Number 79, 1867

Victorian Municipal Directory and Gazette, Arnall & Jackson, Melbourne, 1880-95.

Western Australian Postal Directory, 1906-15.

Maps and drawings

City West Water, *House Cover File*, Plan No. 00035798. (No historic property service file plans of 519 Dryburgh Street survive.)

Crown Lands Office, Map of Melbourne and its Suburbs, 1861. (Copy held at Maps Library, Education Resource Centre, University of Melbourne).

Melbourne Metropolitan Board of Works, Town of North Melbourne Survey Map, Detail Plan No.747 & 742, 1896.

Melbourne Metropolitan Board of Works, Melbourne and North Melbourne, Detail Plan No. 31, 1896.

O'Neill, Hugh, Drawings of proposed renovations at 519 Dryburgh Street, 1969.

Parish plan of Jika Jika (M314/13), Land Victoria.

Subdivision Plans of Crown Allotments 147A & 147B in the Parish of Bairnsdale, Certificate of Title, Volume 1837, Folio 289.

Subdivision Plans LP34460, 28522, Parish of Jika Jika, Land Victoria.

Indexes

Australian Architectural Index, Latrobe Library, State Library of Victoria.

Building Permit Application Index, 1914-2004, Melbourne City Council.

Burchett Index, Latrobe Library, State Library of Victoria.

Manuscripts and typescripts

Certificate of Title for 519 Dryburgh Street, Volume 1130, Folio 225882, Land Victoria.

Character reference for John Langford from inhabitants of Gravesend, 1857, from 'Grandfather Langford's Testimonial', manuscript held by Langford family.

Death and Marriage Certificates, (for Langford family members and occupants of 519 Dryburgh Street), Registry of Births, Deaths and Marriages (Victoria).

Langford, George H, 'Copy of My Grandfather's Testimonial', typescript held by Langford family.

McDonald, Louise, 'Testimonial of Louise Macdonald (Miller)', manuscript held by Maryborough Library.

Melbourne Rate Books 1855-1905.

MS 3895-97, Box 28/5, Rayson, Phillip, Correspondence 1858-1860, Royal Historical Society of Victoria.

MS 12866, Amess, John W. B., Diaries 1887-1900, Manuscripts Collection, State Library of Victoria.

North Melbourne (Hotham) Rate Books 1855-1905.

PROV, VPRS 4030/P/0, Units 2-12, MCC Markets Committee Minutes.

PROV, VPRS 7591/P/2, Unit 503, File 132/452, Proceedings of Inquest of Alfred John Langford.

PROV, VPRS 8600/P/1, Unit 24, Book 426, MMBW Field Survey Notebooks.

PROV, VPRS 763/P/0, Unit 22, File C239, Deeds of Composition (per Robert Langford).

PROV, VPRS 4084/P/0, Unit 2, Volumes 1, MCC Market Rents.

PROV, VPRS 7591/P/2, Unit 222, File 54/782, Probate of William Charles Miller.

PROV, VPRS 28 Series, Probate and Administration Files, (various).

PROV, VPRS 8943/P/1, Units 6-8, Minutes of Council Meetings, North Melbourne (Hotham) Council.

Secondary sources

Books and articles

Adams, John, *Path Among the Years: History of Shire of Bairnsdale*, Bairnsdale Shire Council, Bairnsdale, 1987.

Allan, John (editor), *The Victorian Centenary Book*, Tavistock Press, Melbourne, 1936.

Allom Lovell & Associates, *Fitzroy Town Hall Conservation Management Plan*, report prepared 1996.

Aston, Tilly, *Memoirs of Tilly Aston*, Hawthorn Press, Melbourne, 1946.

Australian Dictionary of Biography, (Volume 3), Melbourne University Press, Carlton, 1978.

Bagot, Alex, *Coppin the Great,* Melbourne University Press, London, 1965.

Barrett, Bernard, *The Inner Suburbs,* Melbourne University Press, Carlton, 1971.

Bate, Weston, *Essential but Unplanned: The Story of Melbourne's Lanes*, City of Melbourne, Melbourne, 1994.

Bate, Weston, *Victorian Gold Rushes*, The Sovereign Hill Museums Association, Ballarat, (second edition), 1999.

Bendigo and District in 1902, The Periodical Publishing Company, Melbourne, 1902.

Benson, James, *A History of Gravesend*, Phillimore, London, 1976.

Blainey, Geoffrey, *The Tyranny of Distance,* Sun Books, Melbourne, 1982.

Brabazon, Elizabeth, *A Month at Gravesend*, Simpkin, Marshall & Co., London, 1864.

Briggs, Asa, *Victorian Cities*, Penguin Books, Ringwood, reprinted 1987.

Brisbane, Katherine, *Entertaining Australia*, Currency Press, Sydney, 1991.

Brown-May, Andrew, *Melbourne Street Life*, Australian Scholarly Publishing, Melbourne, 1998.

Buncle, John, *Experiences of a Victorian Manufacturer*, reprinted from the *North Melbourne Advertiser*, 1889.

Butler, Graeme, *North and West Melbourne Conservation Study*, Volume 9, 1983.

Campbell, Alastair, *John Batman and the Aborigines*, Kibble Books, Malmsbury, 1987.

Cannon, Michael, *Melbourne After the Gold Rush,* Loch Haven Books, Main Ridge, 1993.

Cannon, Michael, *Old Melbourne Town Before the Gold Rushes,* Loch Haven Books, Main Ridge, 1991.

Cannon, Michael, *The Land Boomers*, Melbourne University Press, Carlton, 1973.

Clarke, C. M. H., *A History of Australia*, Volume 4, Melbourne University Press, Carlton, 1978.

Clarke, Michael, *Clarke of Rupertswood 1831-1897,* Australian Scholarly Publishing, Melbourne, 1995.

Cole, Colin E. (editor), *Melbourne Markets 1841-1879,* Melbourne Wholesale Fruit and Vegetable Market Trust, Footscray, 1980.

Davison, Graeme (editor), *The Outcasts of Melbourne,* Allen & Unwin, Sydney, 1985.

Davison, Graeme, *The Rise and Fall of Marvellous Melbourne*, Melbourne University Press, Carlton, 1979.

Diamond, Jared, *Guns, Germs and Steel*, Vintage (Random House), Milson's Point, 1997.

Dowling, Gerard, *The North Story,* Playwright Publishing, Caringbah, 1996.

Dyster, Barrie & Meredith, David, *Australia in the International Economy,* Cambridge University Press, Melbourne, 1990.

Evans, Ian, *Restoring Old Houses,* Sun Books, South Melbourne, 1986.

Fairweather, Don, *Your Friend Alberto Zelman*, The Orchestra, Melbourne, 1984.

Finn, Edmund ('Garryowen'), *The Chronicles of Early Melbourne*, Heritage Publications, reprinted 1976 (first published 1888).

Flett, James, *Dunolly*, Poppet Head Press, Glen Waverley, 1980.

Flett, James, *Maryborough*, The Poppet Head Press, Glen Waverly, 1975.

Freeman, John, *Lights and Shadows of Melbourne Life*, Sampson Low, Marston, Searle, & Rivington, London, 1888.

Giffard, Anne and Greenhill, Basil, *Travelling by Sea in the Nineteenth Century*, Adam & Charles Black, London, 1972.

Gimesy, Oscar, *Built From Nothing*, Building Careers Resource Centre of Australia, Carlton, 1992

Irving, Robert, *The History and Design of the Australian House*, Oxford University Press, Melbourne, 1985.

Leavitt, T. W. H. (editor), *The Jubilee History of Victoria and Melbourne Illustrated*, Volume 1, Duffus Bros. Printers, Melbourne, 1888.

Kehoe, Mary, *The Melbourne Benevolent Asylum*, The Hotham History Project, North Melbourne, 1998.

Kent Town Council, *Gravesend and Neighbourhood*, Cheltenham, 1929.

Korzelinski, Seweryn, *Memoirs of Gold Digging in Australia*, University of Queensland Press, St Lucian, 1979.

Job, Macarthur, *Air Crash*, (Volume 2), Aerospace Publications, Canberra, 1992.

Johnson, Ken, *People and Property in North Melbourne*, Urban Research Unit, Research School of Social Sciences, Australian National University, Canberra, 1974.

Lawrence, W. J., *The Life of Gustavus Vaughan Brooke*, W. & G. Baird, Belfast, 1892.

Lewis, Hilary, *South Parkville*, Second Edition, The Parkville Association, Melbourne, 1996.

Lewis, Miles, *Melbourne: The City's History and Development*, City of Melbourne, Melbourne, 1995.

Lewis, Miles *Physical Investigation of a Building*, National Trust of Australia (Victoria), Melbourne, 1989.

Lockett, Terence, *Collecting Victorian Tiles*, Baron Publishing, Suffolk, 1979.

New Encyclopedia Brittanica, 15th Edition, 1995.

Nicholls, Matthew, *41 Brougham Street North Melbourne and its History*, 1986, (typescript held at Latrobe Library, State Library of Victoria).

O'Hanlon, Seamus, *Together Apart: Boarding House, Hostel and Flat Life in Pre-war Melbourne*, Australian Scholarly Publishing, Melbourne, 2002.

Page, William (editor), *A History of Kent* (Volume 3), The Victoria History of the Counties of England, St Catherine Press, Waterloo, 1932.

Paynting H. H. & Grant, Malcolm, *Victoria Illustrated* 1834-1984, James Flood-Harold Paynting Charity Trust, Melbourne, 1984.

Philip, A. J., *A History of Gravesend*, 1914, Volume 1.

Pierce, Peter, *From Go to Whoa*, Crossbow Publishing, East Melbourne, 1994.

Presland, Gary, *The First Residents of Melbourne's Western Region*, Forrest Hill, 1997.

Reed, John (editor), *When Memory Turns the Key*, The Shire of Romsey History Book Committee, Joval, Bacchus Marsh, 1992.

Robertson, E. Graeme, *Ornamental Cast Iron In Melbourne*, Georgian House, Melbourne, 1967.

Ruhen, Olaf, *Port of Melbourne 1835-1876*, Cassell Australia, Melbourne, 1976.

Sands, Robert, *North Melbourne Town Hall Complex Heritage Assessment and Conservation Management Plan*, report prepared for the City of Melbourne, 1991.

Serle, Geoffrey & Thomson, Kathleen, *A Biographical Register of the Victorian Parliament,* 1851-1900, Australian National University Press, Canberra, 1972.

Shaw, Mary Turner, *Builders of Melbourne*, Cypress Books, Melbourne, 1972.

Smith, James (editor), *The Cyclopedia of Victoria*, (Volume 1), Cyclopedia Co., Melbourne, 1902.

Smyth, Brough, *The Goldfields and Mineral Districts of Victoria,* Government Printer, Melbourne, 1869.

Taylor, Fairlie, *Bid Time Return*, Alpha Books, Sydney, 1977.

Tindale, Norman B., *Aboriginal Tribes of Australia*, ANU Press, Canberra, 1974.

Trevor Budge & Associates, *Macedon Ranges Cultural Heritage and Landscape Study*, Volume 4, 1994.

Turner, Brian, The Australian Terrace House, Angus & Robertson, Sydney, 1995.

Verne, Jules, *On the Track*, Ward, Lock & Co, Melbourne, 1939.

Victoria and its Metropolis, Past and Present, (Volume IIB) McCarron, Bird & Co., Melbourne, 1888.

Warne, Elaine, *Errol Street:The First Hundred Years 1857-1957,* Errol Street Centenary Committee, Melbourne, 1974.

Wells, John, *Gippsland: People, a Place and their Past*, Landmark Press, Drouin, 1986.

Whitehead, Georgina, *Royal Park Cultural Heritage Study*, Report for the City of Melbourne, 1998.

Willis, Barbara, *Footprints: A History of the Shire of Tullaroop*, Shire of Tullaroop, Maryborough, 1988.

List of illustrations

Index